ISBN – 978-0-6487555-6-2
Independently Published

Front Cover Image – Wide Bay Boronia (*Boronia rivularis*)
Back Cover Image – Black She-Oak (*Allocasuarina littoralis*) – male flower spikes
Inside Cover Image – Swamp Banksia (*Banksia robur*) seed cone with open capsules
Inside Back Cover – Satinay (*Syncarpia hillii*)

PREFACE

There are many books which focus on Fraser Island (K'Gari), but few, if any, provide a guide to the plants which inhabit it. This book aims to do just that and is directed at anyone visiting the island who has an interest in the diversity of vegetation species found there, their habitats and survival strategies.

Recent years have seen a vast increase in visitors to Fraser Island (K'Gari). When you visit this very special and unique place, please respect that it has over 700,000 years of history and contains ancient species, some of which are found nowhere else on Earth.

The 94 species included in this book are just a small selection of the total species found throughout Fraser Island (K'Gari). They have been chosen for inclusion as they are familiar species commonly encountered by Fraser Island (K'Gari) visitors. They are also easily identifiable.

The book has been divided into colour-coded chapters based on the island's ecological communities, as recognised by the Queensland Government's Department of Environment and Science. Each chapter includes examples of species found in that specific habitat, with relevant information such as identifying features and general notes.

It is important to note there are species which can be found in more than one specific community, however for the purposes of this book they have only been included in one.

If you are looking for a specific plant and cannot find it in the chapter you thought it would be please check the complete list of species (and their page numbers) at the back of the book. It may overlap communities and be included elsewhere.

Some technical language has been included in the text. These words have been highlighted and their definitions included in a glossary contained at the back of the book.

CONTENTS

Preface	iii.
Introduction	1.
Logging	4.
Fire	7.
Bush Tucker and Bush Medicine	9.
Leaves	12.
The Queen's Commonwealth Canopy	16.
Coastal	18.
Mangroves	31.
Tall Eucalypt Forest	37.
Rainforest	46.
Mixed Forest	70.
Wallum	95.
Glossary of Terms	127.
Index	132.
Bibliography	136.

INTRODUCTION

Fraser Island (K'Gari) is arguably one of the most spectacular, intriguing, and popular islands in the world. Situated off the coast of Hervey Bay and approximately 300 km north of Brisbane, it is the world's largest sand island, stretching 123 km in length and covering an estimated area of 166,038 ha.

Fraser Island (K'Gari) contains only three rocky outcrops of interbedded volcanic and sedimentary rocks from the Mesozoic Era (252–66 mya) and Tertiary Period (66–2.6 mya). These are Indian Head, Middle Rocks and Waddy Point. It is these three sites which are primarily responsible for the formation of the Island.

These outcrops acted as an anchor point for **alluvial** sands and sediments originating from the Blue Mountains, part of Australia's Great Dividing Range. These sands and sediments were carried in a northerly direction by strong oceanic currents and waves where they began to accumulate and form the beginnings of what would later become known as Fraser Island (K'Gari).

Both Fraser Island (K'Gari) and it's southern counterpart, Cooloola, are remnants of sandmasses which once stretched 30km further east. Dune-building has continued episodically due to changes in sea level. This has resulted in a sequence of over-lapping dune systems estimated to be more than 700,000 years old, and some of the oldest on record.

In December 1992 Fraser Island (K'Gari) was inscribed on the World Heritage list in recognition of its internationally significant features. These include ancient dune systems and lakes, as well as diverse species of **endemic** flora and fauna.

Specifically, in addition to these important values, the island contains extraordinary landscapes such as sandblows, striking coloured sand cliffs and rainforests growing in nutrient poor conditions.

In response to the lack of nutrients throughout the island there are obvious and distinctive changes to plant communities.

Nine dune systems have been identified, with the oldest system occurring on the west coast. Here, the B Horizon of the soil profile, which contains the nutrient layer, is too deep for plants to access.

As a result, trees are sparser and have lower canopy cover, with many utilising mallee growth forms (growing multiple stems from an underground **lignotuber**).

Towards the middle of the island the soil profile is well developed. Here, large rainforest species are supported by the nutrient dense B Horizon, which is thick and deep.

The eastern side is considered to be the youngest part of the island. There is no developed soil profile and as such no, or very little, nutrient availability. Here, **pioneer species** dominate the landscape and help to stabilise the foreshore for the secondary species which follow.

There is no doubt the extraordinary natural features of Fraser Island (K'Gari) have seen it become a major drawcard for visitors. This, in itself, presents many challenges in ensuring that the conservation of these values are balanced with opportunities for enjoyment and education.

LOGGING

In 1842, whilst surveying the local area, pioneer and builder, Andrew Petrie, discovered vast stands of timber on Fraser Island (K'Gari). Specifically, his interest lay in the Kauri Pine (*Agathis robusta*), which became the initial focus of the Island's logging era in 1863. Due to the heavy logging of this species, there are very few examples of mature stands remaining today.

An attempt at **re-afforestation**, through the planting of 28,000 Kauri Pine seedlings amongst thick scrub, occurred between 1883-1884. Kauri Pines, however, are not a shade tolerant species. Thus, the planting was unsuccessful.

In addition to Kauri Pines, other species were logged for characteristics which made them attractive for certain uses. Specifically, Tallow Wood (*Eucalyptus microcorys*), Blackbutt (*Eucalyptus pilularis*), Hoop Pine (*Araucaria cunninghamii*), White Beech (*Gmelina leichhardtii*), and Brush Box (*Lophostemon confertus*) were removed, however it was the Satinay (*Syncarpia hillii*) which proved the most robust for construction purposes.

With its marine borer resistance and 200 year life expectancy Satinay timber is considered suitable for the construction of structures such as jetties, bridges and wharves. The pylons of the Kingfisher Bay Resort jetty, on the western side of the island and Hervey Bay's Urangan Pier are built from Satinay.

Found primarily on Fraser Island (K'Gari) and throughout small pockets of the adjoining Cooloola region, it has a very limited range. It continued to be logged until 1991, and now has limited availability.

Until 1905, bullocks were used to move logs around the island, after which steam locomotives were introduced. The locomotives were fueled by timber off cuts and caused numerous fires as a result of the sparks they emitted. In 1937, the locomotives were replaced with vehicles.Felled timber was transported to the Maryborough mill for processing. Initially, softwoods were rafted up the Mary River, however later on when the denser hardwoods were taken, barges were used.

In 1918, Mr H. McKenzie, a NSW timber merchant, built the first and only timber mill on Fraser Island (K'Gari) at North White Cliffs, after his company, McKenzie Ltd, purchased the rights to log 4000 hectares of the island over 10 years. In 1925, the business was considered no longer economically viable and ceased operation. Remnants of McKenzie's Jetty still stand at the site of the sawmill, south from Kingfisher Bay Resort.

In 1920, Central Station became the site of a forestry camp, which developed into a busy and self-sufficient community. Houses, stables and sheds were built, fruit trees and vegetable gardens were planted and a school was established for the children of the forestry workers.

Logging officially ceased in November 1991, after a Commission of Inquiry (The Fitzgerald Inquiry) was conducted. This resulted from increasing pressure from conservation groups to halt logging on the island due to unsustainable environmental impacts such as changes to forest structure, loss of soil, invasion of weeds and impacts on wildlife.

Photo credit Peter Meyer Photography

FIRE

The Australian landscape is dynamic and ever-changing, an endless cycle of drought, flood and fire. Fire, in particular, is an important aspect of the ecological characteristics of Australia's environment. For thousands of years Traditional Owners have used fire as part of their management of Country, in addition to using it as a hunting tool.

In response, native species have had to adapt and devise ways to cope with the harshness they are constantly exposed to. Many species have developed unique ways to not only survive exposure to fire, but to use it to their advantage.

For many species of Australian plants fire is a necessary part of their reproductive cycle. Some species require fire to stimulate the opening of their woody capsules in order to release the seeds contained within, or for their dormant seeds to begin germinating. These species also rely on the nutrient-dense ash left behind, which provides nourishment for young shoots and new growth.

Other species however, utilise their **epicormic buds**, or underground **lignotuber** to re-establish after fire by drawing on the nutrients they store.

As the managing agency of Fraser Island (K'Gari), the Queensland Parks and Wildlife Service are responsible for undertaking annual controlled rotational burns across the island. These burns occur in a mosaic pattern of burnt and unburnt areas across the island, which are used to help maintain biological diversity, restore and regenerate degraded areas, control and eradicate pest species and reduce fuel loads.

BUSH TUCKER AND BUSH MEDICINE

Many of the plants of Fraser Island (K'Gari) were used by local Traditional Owners, the Butchulla people, as sources of food and medicine. For thousands of years their vast knowledge of which plants are edible and which ones are useful as remedies for ailments has been handed down through generations.

Additionally, European settlers found many uses for the diverse range of plant species they encountered during the early days of colonisation, although much of what we know today stems from the knowledge of the Traditional Owners.

Bush tucker is now widely used in contemporary cooking and, indeed, is a staple of many modern restaurants and cuisine. Our knowledge of bush medicine, however, is continuing to evolve thanks to ongoing scientific research into plant compounds and their role in modern-day medicine.

Following is a list of uses for a multitude of plant species found on Fraser Island (K'Gari), with several serving purposes for both bush tucker and bush medicine. Further information relating to the uses of specific plants can also be found within the species profile pages.

Please note the details relating to bush tucker and bush medicine contained within this book are for information purposes only and do not constitute a recommendation to use them without proper knowledge and care. Please also note the plants of Fraser Island (K'Gari) are protected and should not be damaged or removed from the island.

Hop Bush (*Dodonaea triquetra*) – Used by the Butchulla people to relieve toothache and stings. Early European settlers used the fruits to make beer.

Prickly Broom Heath (*Monotoca scoparia*) – Traditional Owners ate the fruit (raw) and only when it was white, avoiding it when green.

Flax Lily (*Dianella revoluta*) – The berries are edible, as well as the base of the leaves.

Black She-Oak (*Allocasuarina littoralis*) – The dark, sticky sap produced by this species was collected and boiled down to make a jelly-like food.

Pandanus Screw Palm (*Pandanus tectorius*) – Traditional Owners chewed the inner core of young leaves to cure stomach cramps and diarrhoea. The woody wedges of the fruit were pulped to make an alcoholic drink.

Grasstrees (*Xanthorrhoea spp.*) – Many parts of this plant were utilised by the Butchulla people. The core at the base of the plant is starchy and was eaten raw or roasted. The flowering stalk was used to make a sweet drink by dipping it into water.

Native Pig Face (*Carpobrotus glaucesens*) – The fruit was a popular food source for Traditional Owners due to its salty strawberry-like flavour. The leaves are also edible, but not pleasant. Juice taken from the leaves was used as a treatment for stings.

Picabeen Palm (*Archontophoenix cunninghammii*) – The fruit of this species is edible, although not pleasant. New shoots were eaten either raw or cooked. The leaves were used as a cast for broken bones.

Cypress Pine (*Callitris columellaris*) – As a treatment for sores and scabies, the leaves were finely ground and boiled in water. This mixture was also rubbed over the chest to relieve coughing.

Eucalyptus spp. – The leaves of these species were used to make a mouthwash to ease toothache. They were also chewed into a pulp and applied to sore eyes.

Lemon-Scented Tea Tree (*Leptospermum liversidgei*) The natural insect-repelling properties of this species made it useful to both Traditional Owner and early European settlers. The Europeans also used the leaves to brew an infusion of lemon tea.

LEAVES

Leaves are one of the most important features of plants, with their primary function being to undertake **photosynthesis**.

Leaves contain a variety of features which are important to consider when attempting to identify a plant. These include the margin of the leaf, veins, **midrib**, the tip and the base. In addition, the arrangement of the leaf is crucial to identification. Leaves which are 'simple' are not divided into smaller units, called leaflets, and are instead 'whole'.

This is in contrast to 'compound' leaves, which consist of several distinct leaflets joined to a single stem (petiole). **Compound leaves** can be further classified as 'pinnate' or 'palmate'. The leaflets of pinnate leaves are located on each side of their common stem (petiole). These leaflets can also be further divided into smaller leaflets, a characteristic called 'bipinnate'.

The leaflets of palmate leaves differ in that they are attached to, and radiate out from, a central point at the top of the stem (petiole). Leaf arrangement also refers to the way it grows on the stem, such as alternate (a single leaf attached at a **node**), opposite (2 leaves attached at a **node**), and in whorls (3 or more leaves attached at a **node**).

There are many different types and characteristics of leaves, however the shape of a leaf, in conjunction with the reproductive features (flowers, seeds), is one of the most useful in identifying individual species. Examples of leaf arrangement and shape are given below:

Leaf Arrangement:

| Simple | Compound (pinnate) | Compound (palmate) |

Encyclopaedia Brittanica (2019)

Alternate   Opposite   Whorled

Encyclopaedia Brittanica (2019)

Leaf Shape:

Elliptic The broadest part is the middle, with the ends narrowing equally. Total length is approximately twice as long as it is wide.

Woombye (*Phebalium woombye*)

Lanceolate These leaves are significantly longer than they are wide. The widest part occurs below the middle. The end tapers to a point.

Lemon Myrtle (*Backhousia citriodora*)

Linear The margins are parallel and the leaf is more than 12 times longer than it is wide.

Small-Leaved Geebung (*Persoonia virgata*)

Needle-like These leaves resemble needles.

Prickly Moses (*Acacia ulicifolia*)

Oblong These leaves are rectangle-shaped, with rounded corners. They are twice as long as they are wide.

Yellow Tea Tree (*Leptospermum polygalifolium*)

Obovate These leaves are similar in shape to an egg. The broader end of the leaf is furthest from the stem.

Native Gardenia (*Atractocarpus fitzlanii*)

Ovate These leaves are similar in shape to an egg. The broader end of the leaf is nearest the stem.

Kauri Pine (*Agathis robusta*)

THE QUEEN'S COMMONWEALTH CANOPY

In 2018 the forests of Fraser Island (K'Gari) were officially dedicated to the Queen's Commonwealth Canopy initiative, with HRH the Duke of Sussex officially unveiling a plaque located at Pile Valley.

The Queen's Commonwealth Canopy project was launched in 2015, with the aim of establishing a Commonwealth-wide network of research and conservation efforts, in addition to preserving protected and sustainable forest areas in perpetuity in the name of Her Majesty. To date, 42 of the 53 Commonwealth countries have contributed 90 projects to this initiative (Australia has dedicated 3 projects). These projects include programs involving management, rehabilitation and conservation, and covers over 78,500 km^2 of native forest areas.

The Royal Commonwealth Society is responsible for leading the Queen's Commonwealth Canopy, in conjunction with The Commonwealth Forestry Association and Cool Earth. It is hoped that eventually the remaining Commonwealth countries will engage with the project and provide the final and pivotal ecological links across the Commonwealth, resulting in positive and long-lasting benefits for the forests and all who rely on, or enjoy, them.

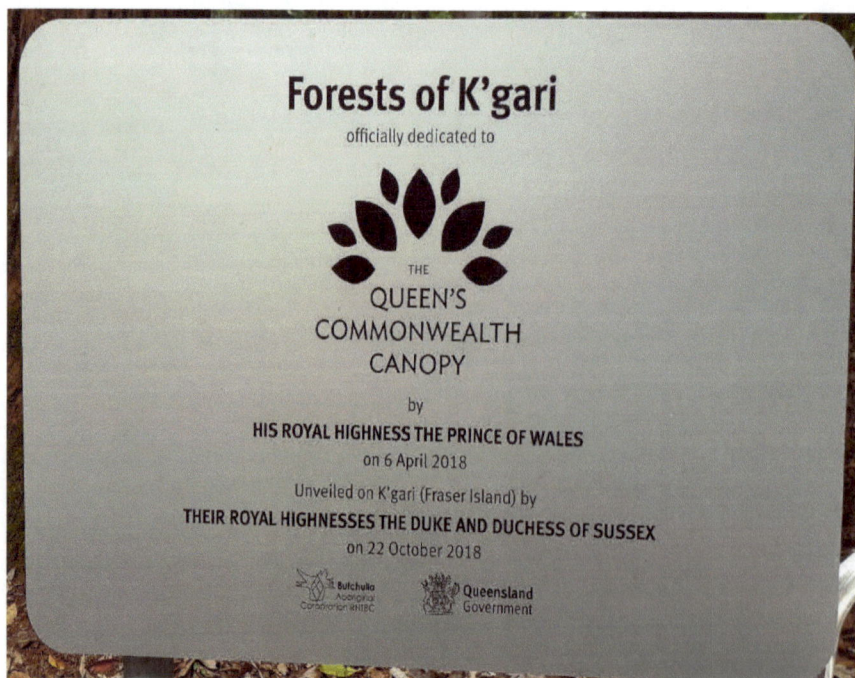

Forests of K'gari
officially dedicated to

THE
QUEEN'S
COMMONWEALTH
CANOPY

by
HIS ROYAL HIGHNESS THE PRINCE OF WALES
on 6 April 2018
Unveiled on K'gari (Fraser Island) by
THEIR ROYAL HIGHNESSES THE DUKE AND DUCHESS OF SUSSEX
on 22 October 2018

Butchulla
Aboriginal
Corporation #NTBC   Queensland
Government

COASTAL

Coastal communities are dynamic places. They are forever transforming, thanks to the tides, waves and winds that act upon them. They are also home to a diverse array of specialised plants adapted to living in very harsh conditions.

Beaches form when sediment, usually sand, is transported by waves and deposited in a place where it can accumulate. The sand particles on beaches, however, do not stay in one place. They are constantly in a state of flux thanks to wind and the process of longshore drift.

Water particles move up a beach face at an angle with wave direction, but return directly down the slope. Sand picked up by the incoming wave is washed up the beach and returned seaward a small distance down the beach in the direction of the waves. Successive waves move sand progressively along the beach, a process known as longshore, or littoral, drift. The path the sand particles follow is a zigzag pattern. The different zones of beaches are easily identifiable as follows:

Sublittoral (subtidal) - the continental shelf floor that is permanently covered by water.

Littoral (intertidal) - the region between the low tide line and the high tide line which is covered with water during only part of each tidal cycle.

Supralittoral (splash) - the region above the high tide line that is covered by water only when large storm waves, high tides or storm surges reach the coast.

The western coastal communities are the oldest on Fraser Island (K'Gari) and differ greatly to the eastern side of the island in terms of wave, tidal and current activity. The eastern beaches of the island are exposed to the open ocean.

Therefore, these areas experience larger waves and stronger currents than those on the western side, which display calmer conditions due to the protection afforded by the island itself.

Additionally, the forces of **erosion** and **accretion** are constantly acting on all coasts of Fraser Island (K'Gari). **Erosion** is a natural and essential process which helps to build and shape beaches and dunes.

The endless movement of sand particles contributes to the **ecology** and **morphology** of coastal systems and ensures that (on a particulate scale, at least) from one day to the next Fraser Island's (K'Gari) beaches are never the same.

In response to the differing coastal conditions of the island, the vegetation found on the western side is vastly different to that on the eastern side. Mangroves and low-lying creepers dominate the western coastline, whilst Spinifex Grass, Coastal She-Oaks and Coastal Banksias are more commonly seen within the eastern dune systems.

Coastal plants survive in harsh and hostile environments which require them to adapt to conditions such as low nutrient availability, sea/salt spray, high wind velocity and reduced access to fresh water.

Some of the adaptations these species have developed in order to survive here include; developing tough leathery leaves which reduce water loss, producing needle-like leaves which minimise surface area and water loss, fine hairs on leaves and stems to trap and reduce water loss. Species which are smaller (eg. ground covers) can also better tolerate wind conditions and sand blasting.

Additionally, many plant species rely on animals such as birds and insects for assistance with the reproductive process. However, plants found in coastal communities primarily utilise wind and ocean currents for pollen and seed dispersion.

It has been calculated that a wave can disturb sand to a depth of 40% of its height (ie. 40 cm for a 1 m wave). This means that organic nutrients are continually being re-suspended and little is retained in the sand. This has vast implications for the vegetation which inhabit coastal areas and explains the successive establishment of **pioneer** and secondary species in these communities.

Beach Evening Primrose
(*Oenothera drummondii*)

Other names: Evening Primrose; Coastal Primrose

Identifying features: The Beach Primrose is a **perennial** herbaceous groundcover species which grows to approximately 60 cm in height.

The leaves and stems of this species are densely covered in hairs, giving the plant a silvery-green appearance. Leaf shape varies between **obovate**, **elliptic** and narrow-**lanceolate**, with leaves measuring between 2-14 cm in length and 5-20 mm wide.

Flowering occurs between spring and autumn, when bright yellow, 4-petaled flowers appear. Flowers are relatively large, with each petal measuring between 2-4 cm long. The fruit of the Beach Primrose is cylindrical in shape (3-5.5 cm long, 2-3 mm wide) and densely covered in soft hair.

Each capsule contains multiple brown seeds 1.1-1.7 mm in length.

General notes: The Beach Primrose is an introduced species, originating in northern Mexico and south eastern USA (eg. Florida, Texas, South Carolina). It is considered an environmental weed within Queensland, however there are conflicting opinions on the extent of its environmental impact within Australia. It is thought the Beach Primrose was introduced to Australia through ship ballast water.

Beach Spinifex
(*Spinifex sericeus*)

Other names: Hairy Spinifex; Sand Spinifex

Identifying features: Beach Spinifex is a stout, **dioecious perennial** grass, producing leaves between 10-40 cm in length. Leaves appear silver on the upper surface, with the lower surface containing a covering of short, silky hairs.

Male plants produce clusters of pale brown flowers approximately 5cm long. Female plants produce large, round, straw-coloured seed heads containing spikes up to 10-15 cm in length.

General notes: Spinifex is one of the most common species seen on the frontal dunes of exposed coastal foreshores and are one of the most important found here.

Beach Spinifex is a **pioneer** sand-stabilising species. It is salt tolerant and able to tolerate the large amounts of wind-blown sand which blanket it.

The structure of Spinifex helps to reduce wind velocity on the surface of the sand and traps any sand which blows over the plant. This helps to stabilise the dune system and aids in the dune building process.

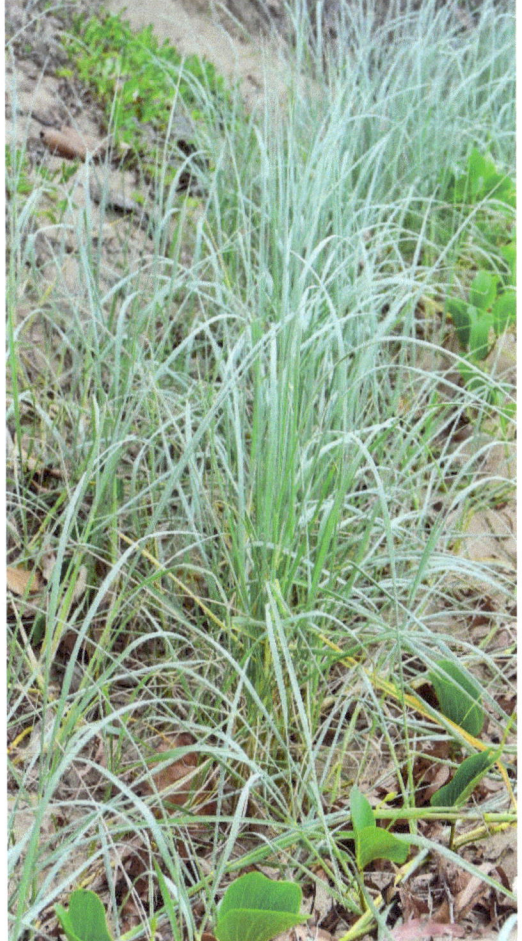

Coastal Banksia
(*Banksia integrifolia*)

Identifying features: Coastal Banksia is a small to medium sized tree, growing up to 9 m tall. The dense canopy forms from numerous short branches.

Leaves are **oblong** in shape, approximately 16 cm long, broad at the tip and dark green on the upper surface with a light green **midrib**. The under surface is white with yellow-green patterns caused by veins. Young leaves are serrated but become smooth as they mature.

The flower heads are cylindrical in shape and up to 12 cm long. The green buds turn yellow as they open. The flowers are arranged spirally.

The brown-black woody cones of this species are between 8 and 12 cm long and contain multiple seed capsules housing 1-2 winged seeds.

General notes: Banksias are **endemic** to Australia, and are therefore found nowhere else in the world.

Banksias were discovered by Botanists Joseph Banks and Daniel Solander in 1770 during Captain James Cook's voyage on HMS Endeavour (1768-1771).

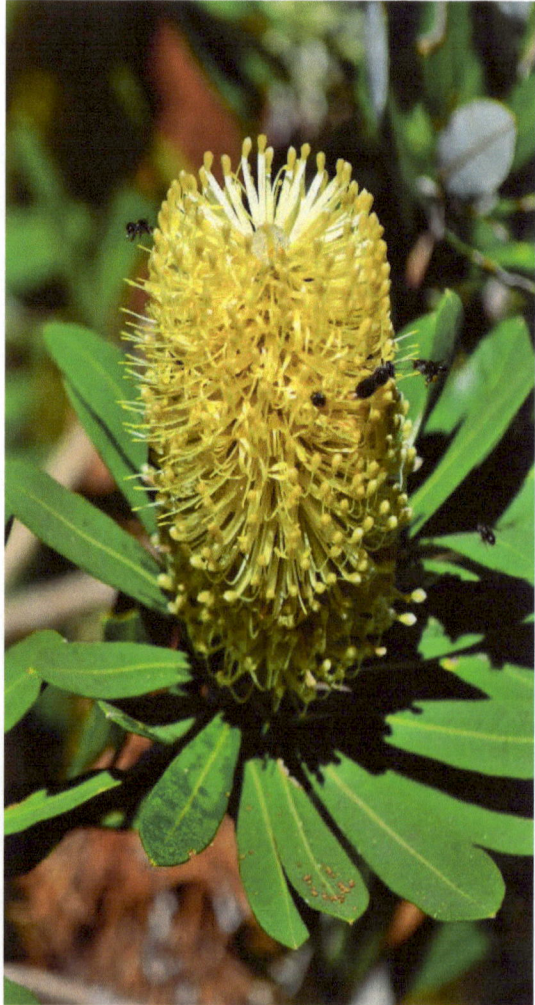

Coastal Jack Bean
(*Canavalia rosea*)

Other names: Beach Bean; Wild Jack Bean

Identifying features: The Coastal Jack Bean is a trailing or climbing herbaceous **perennial** vine, with stems measuring up to 3 m in length and 2 cm in diameter.

The leaves of this species are bright green in colour and form a 3-lobed **compound** variation, with each leaflet (lobe) between 4 and 10 cm in diameter. Pink to purple-coloured pea-like flowers (see *Common Aotus*) between 2-3 cm in length appear sporadically year-round.

Fleshy pods, measuring 10-15 cm in length, contain multiple brown bean-shaped seeds. As the pods age they become increasingly woody and ridged.

Upon maturity the pods release the seeds, which are dispersed by ocean currents.

General notes: When exposed to high temperatures due to direct sunlight, the leaflets will fold up. This helps to reduce the surface area of the leaflets exposed to the sunlight and reduces **transpiration**.

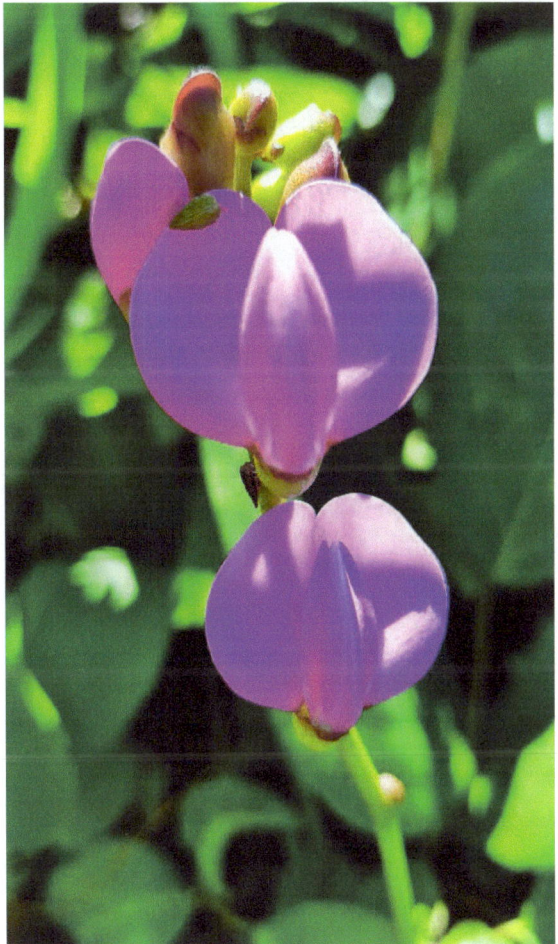

Coastal She-Oak
(*Casuarina equisetifolia*)

Other name: Horsetail She-Oak

Identifying features: Coastal She-Oaks are distinctive trees growing between 6-12 m high. The lower trunk of this species has rough dark-coloured bark. Fine green-grey branchlets form needle-like structures which display a drooping arrangement.

Male plants produce small flowers on the end of the branchlets, while female plants produce cylindrical cones which increase in size after pollination. These cones contain small, winged, brown seeds which are released upon maturation.

General notes: The downwards hanging position of the needles allows the plant to reduce water lost through **transpiration** by pointing away from, and reducing the surface area exposed to, direct sunlight.

The term '*Casuarina*' comes from the Latin word '*casuarinus*', which means 'like a cassowary'. This is because the drooping branchlets of these species are thought to resemble cassowary feathers.

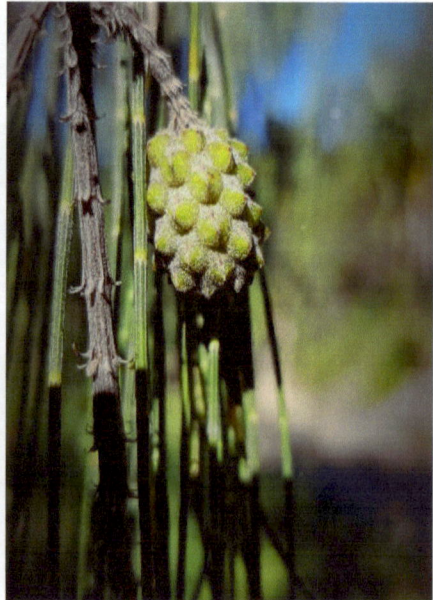

Goat's Foot Vine (convolvulus)
(*Ipomoea pes-caprae*)

Other name: Beach Morning Glory

Identifying features: Goat's Foot Vine is a spreading **perennial** species which produces stems up to 8 m long. The bright green leaves are between 3-14 cm in length, roughly oval in shape and are often notched at the tip.

The flowers of this species are pink-purple in colour, 3-7 cm long and bell-shaped. Seeds are produced in a brown pod between 12-15 cm long.

General notes: This species gets its name from the shape of its leaves, which are thought to resemble the foot of a goat. Interestingly, *'pes-caprae'* is a Latin term which means 'foot of a goat'.

The leaf density of this species is usually sparse in exposed areas, however it will increase in protected areas.

Goat's Foot Vine is a **pioneering species** which helps to stabilise sand dunes. It is often found growing near Beach Spinifex.

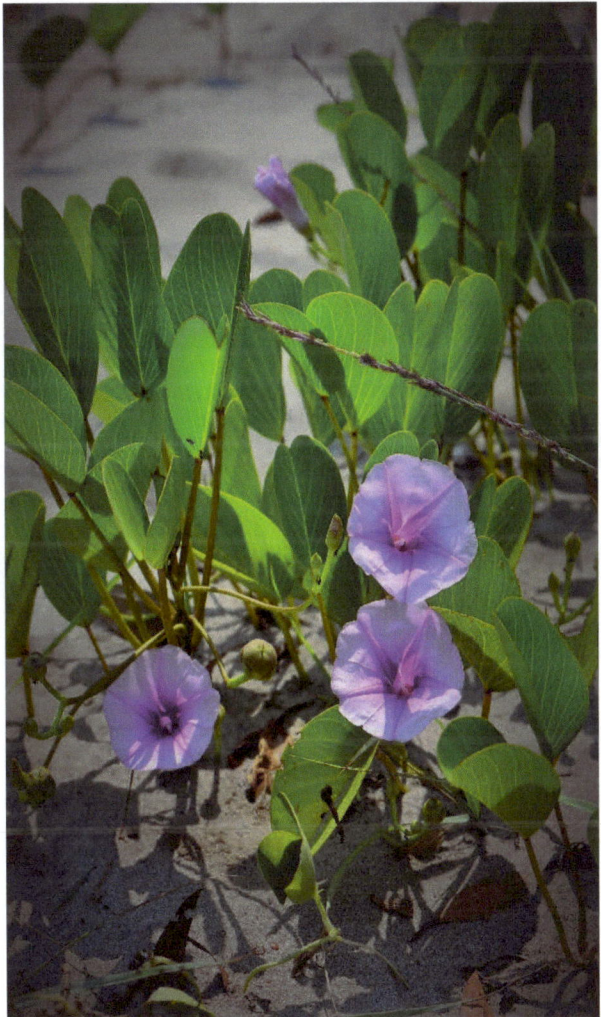

Knobby Club-Rush
(*Ficinia nodosa*)

Other names: Knobby Club-Sedge; Knotted Club-Rush

Identifying features: The Knobby Club-Rush is a clumping **perennial** herb, which grows from a stout **rhizome**. The erect stems of this species reach between 20-90 cm in height and 1-2 mm in diameter and are sheathed by the reduced leaves, which are orange-brown in colour.

Flowering occurs from November to March, when brown globular-shaped flower heads appear, with each flower head between 10-20 mm in diameter and covered in numerous spikelets.

The fruit it produces is a small, smooth, black, shiny and irregularly-shaped nut (approximately 1 mm long, 0.7 mm diameter).

General notes: The Knobby Club-Rush relies on wind for pollination and dispersal of its seeds.

This species is useful for restoring dune systems. Its extensive root system helps to bind the sand and provides stability.

The scientific name of this species was previously known as *Isolepsis nodosa*. It is now considered more closely related to the South African species of *Ficinia*.

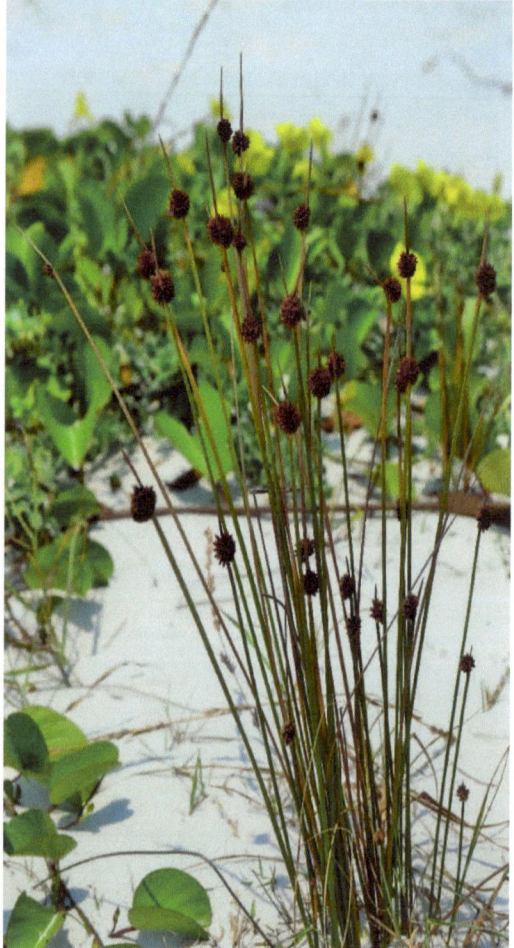

Native Pig Face
(*Carpobrotus glaucesens*)

Other names: Coastal Pig Face; Angular Pig Face

Identifying features: Native Pig Face is a creeping succulent **perennial** species which produces stems up to 2 m long. Numerous leafy upright branches protrude from the stems, with the fleshy, triangular-shaped leaves varying in length from 4-10 cm. Younger leaves appear bluish-green, becoming pinkish-red with age.

The flowers of this species are a deep pink-purple with a yellow centre and are 4-6 cm in width.

General notes: This species gets its name from the centre of the flower, which is thought to resemble the face of a pig. The fruit is succulent and edible, containing small, brown seeds. When ripe, it falls from the plant.

Native Pig Face is a secondary stabiliser, appearing once the **pioneer species**, such as Beach Spinifex and Goat's Foot Vine, have established and improved growing conditions for other species.

Pandanus Screw Palm
(*Pandanus tectorius*)

Identifying features: Pandanus Screw Palms are small trees which can grow up to approximately 8 m in height. The tree is held upright and firmly anchored to the ground by sturdy prop roots.

Leaves are between 90-150 cm long and 5-7 cm wide. They are light green in colour and arranged spirally on the stems of the tree. Pronounced scarring occurs when the leaves fall from the tree.

There are separate male and female plants for this species, but only the female plants produce the large, distinctive pineapple-like fruit. Male plants produce flowers which resemble corncobs.

General notes: The waxy cuticle of the leaves of the Pandanus help prevent water loss by creating a barrier and reducing the amount of water lost through **transpiration**.

Pandanus Screw Palms are a secondary colonising plant. They help to stabilise dune systems and provide protection for hind dune plants by acting as a wind break.

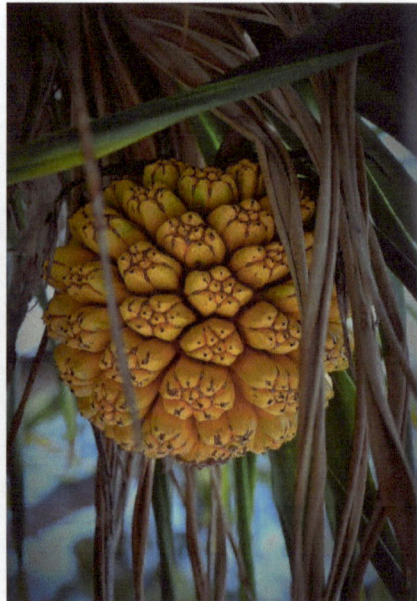

Twining Guinea Flower
(*Hibbertia scandens*)

Other names: Snake Vine; Climbing Guinea Flower

Identifying features: Twining Guinea Flower is an **evergreen perennial** creeper which forms long stems over dune systems.

The upper surface of the leaves of this species are dark and glossy, with the underside whitish in colour and covered with soft hair. Their length is 3-8 cm and width is 3 cm.

Golden yellow flowers measuring 5-7 cm in diameter produce an unpleasant odour. The 5 petals of this species are 2-3 cm long and notched. The fruit of this species is round (2 cm diameter) and contains several red-brown seeds.

General notes: Twining Guinea Flower is one of approximately 150 *Hibbertia* species found only in Australia.

Similarly to other species such as Native Pig Face, the Twining Guinea Flower is a secondary stabilising species.

MANGROVES

Mangroves are plants adapted to life in shallow, muddy, brackish waters, however the word 'mangrove' can also be used to describe the habitat in which the plant lives.

Mangrove forests are diverse communities, which grow in the intertidal zone of coastal rivers, bays and estuaries and are frequently subjected to fluctuations in salinity and temperature, as well as nutrients and oxygen availability.

The conditions they tolerate are much harsher than those of other species, making mangroves unique in their ability to survive in such a dynamic environment. Due to variation of tolerance by different species, distribution patterns occur; this is known as zonation.

For example, species less tolerant of saline conditions are often found growing higher in the intertidal zone (landward side), or in areas where there is considerable freshwater input.

More saline tolerant species are found in the lower intertidal areas. These species can also be found in areas where there is minimal tidal influence but increased evaporation from the soil. This creates **hypersaline** soil, which at times is saltier than seawater.

Mangroves don't need salt in their environment to survive, but research shows they grow best in water which is 50% fresh and 50% salt.

Many mangrove species use their extensive and intricate root system to filter the salt from their system, and some species can remove approximately 90% of the salt in seawater this way. They can also remove it through special salt glands in their leaves.

If you look closely at the leaf of a mangrove you can often see tiny salt crystals on the surface. Some mangroves concentrate the salt in their bark, or in older leaves, which take the salt with them when they fall off.

Mangroves generally have thick waxy leaves or dense hairs on their surface to reduce the amount of water lost through **transpiration**. Thick succulent leaves allow the plant to store water in their fleshy internal tissues.

All plants require oxygen in order to grow and survive. As mangroves generally grow in muddy, **anaerobic** environments they have had to devise ways to adapt to a harsh environment most other plant species are not exposed to.

As such, some mangrove species have devised specialised structures called **pneumatophores**. These are above ground roots, which are filled with spongy tissue.

The surrounding bark has holes which allows oxygen to be transferred to the below ground root system. They also provide structural support for the plant.

There are 4 types of **pneumatophore** – stilt/prop, snorkel/peg, knee and ribbon/plank. Knee and ribbon **pneumatophores** are sometimes combined with buttress roots at the base of the tree to provide extra support.

Mangroves form the interface between marine and terrestrial environments, and consequently animals from both habitats can be found within the mangrove system. This includes crabs, prawns, snakes, flying foxes, birds and saltwater crocodiles.

The Australian Institute of Marine Science (AIMS) estimates that around 75% of all commercially caught fish species spend at least part of their life cycle in a mangrove community. They are frequently utilised by fish as nurseries and therefore play a vital role in the survival and sustainability of future fish stocks.

Worldwide there are 69 recognised species of mangrove, 37 of which inhabit Queensland, with nine species found on Fraser Island (K'Gari).

The three most commonly encountered species on Fraser Island (K'Gari) are described on the following pages.

Grey Mangrove
(Avicennia marina)

Other name: White Mangrove

Identifying features: Grey Mangroves can reach heights of approximately 10 metres and have peg/snorkel, above-ground roots. Their leaves are light green and approximately 10 cm in length, with a silvery-grey under surface containing special glands for secreting excess salt.

The bark of this species is smooth, grey-white to green, which sometimes has a flaky appearance. It produces small, pale, orange flowers and fruits which are almond sized, green and slightly furry.

General notes: Grey mangroves have a high tolerance for saline conditions and are commonly found on the seaward edge of mangrove systems.

They are the most widely distributed mangrove species in Australia, mainly due to its tolerance of cool conditions.

Orange Mangrove
(*Bruguiera gymnorhiza*)

Other name: Large-Leafed Orange Mangrove

Identifying features: Orange Mangroves can grow up to 7 m in height. They can appear either as shrubs or small trees. The trunk of this species is often buttressed, with thick 'knee' roots found around the base of the tree. The bark of the Orange Mangrove is grey-brown, hard and roughly fissured.

The smooth, glossy leaves are **obovate** to **elliptic** in shape. Leaf length varies between 10-25 cm, with width up to 7 cm.

Colouration of the upper leaf surface is dark green, with the lower pale green. The stalks of the leaves of this species have a red tinging.

Flowering occurs from winter to summer, when solitary creamy-red cup-shaped flowers appear. Each flower measures between 3-4 cm in length from which a fleshy **propagule** (15-25 cm) emerges.

General notes: The scientific *'gymnorhiza'* comes from the Greek 'gymno' (which means 'naked') and 'rhiza' (meaning 'root'), a reference to its exposed knee roots.

Red Mangrove
(*Rhizophora stylosa*)

Identifying features: Red Mangroves can grow up to 20 m in height. Their root system is the distinctive prop root.

Leaf length is approximately 10 cm with a lighter green under surface covered with brown speckles. The leaves are arranged in clumps at the end of the branches.

Red Mangroves have rough bark, which varies in colour from brown to dark grey. This species produces small white flowers, which are pollinated by wind or insects. **Propagules** are 1-2 cm in diameter, 20-40 cm long and tapered at one end.

General notes: This is probably the most well-known mangrove species due to its distinguishing root system and widespread distribution.

Due to its high tolerance of saline conditions, Red Mangroves are generally found in the lower intertidal zone, where its roots become submerged during high tides.

TALL EUCALYPT FOREST

Eucalypt trees are a true Australian icon, after having originally evolved from rainforest species. Over time they have become adapted to ever-increasing nutrient-poor conditions and exposure to the regular fires and drought which form part of the Australian landscape.

Almost all of the approximately 900 species of eucalypt identified are found nowhere else, with estimates suggesting that ninety-two million hectares of Australian native forest area is comprised of eucalypt forest.

'Eucalypt' is a collective term, used to refer to several groups of closely related woody plants. Species from the *Eucalyptus*, *Corymbia* and *Angophora* groups commonly occur in these communities.

The vegetation found here is referred to as 'sclerophyll' forest, a reference to the tough, thick and waxy leaves produced by these species. Leaves such as these are considered an adaptation to dry conditions due to the plants ability to quickly recover during favourable conditions, and their capacity to resist permanent damage from wilting.

The waxy coating and the vertical hang of the leaves help eucalypt species reduce the amount of water lost as a result of **transpiration** by providing a barrier to water loss and reducing the amount of surface area exposed to sunlight.

The leaves of eucalypts contain many oil glands, which make them highly combustible. Fire is important to many species of Australian plants, including eucalypts, as a means of releasing the seeds contained inside their woody capsules. The nutrient-dense ash left behind provides ideal conditions for these seeds to begin germinating.

In addition to releasing their stored seeds, fire promotes new growth across eucalypt species due to the **epicormic buds** contained beneath their bark, which remain dormant until they are activated (for example, by fire). This ensures a plant can survive, even if all its leaves are gone.

Blackbutt
(*Eucalyptus pilularis*)

Identifying features: The Blackbutt is a tall forest tree which can grow up to 60 m in height. This species is easily identified by the dark, spongy, fibrous bark on the lower half of the tree and the smooth whitish wood which forms the upper trunk and branches.

The seed capsules of Blackbutts are small and ball shaped. Flowering occurs mainly during summer and autumn, occasionally in spring.

General notes: The globular-shaped seeds of the blackbutt give rise to its scientific name, as '*pilula*' is Latin for 'little ball'.

On Fraser Island (K'Gari) this species is commonly seen around the fringes of rainforest areas, as well as Lake McKenzie, Lake Allom, Eli Creek and Kingfisher Bay Resort.

The quality of the timber produced by Blackbutts have made it a highly sought after species. Blackbutt timber has been used extensively in general construction, such as walkways and decking.

Moreton Bay Ash
(*Corymbia tessellaris*)

Other name: Carbeen

Identifying features: The Moreton Bay ash is a small to medium sized tree growing up to approximately 30 m in height and 1 m diameter. It has dark grey tessellated bark covering the lower 4 metres of its trunk, while the surface of the upper trunk is smooth and white or pale grey in colour.

The leaves of this species are between 12-18 cm in length, up to 2 cm wide and **lanceolate**-shaped, with colouration ranging from green to green-grey. Veins are yellowish in colour and prominent. Clusters of white flowers appear during spring and summer.

General notes: The scientific name '*tessellaris*' comes from Latin and means 'tessellated'. This is in reference to the rough square bark on the lower trunk of this species.

Narrow-Leaved Scribbly Gum
(*Eucalyptus racemosa*)

Identifying features: The Narrow-Leaved Scribbly Gum is a small to medium sized evergreen tree, growing up to 20 m tall. It has greyish bark, which is regularly shed to reveal smooth light-coloured bark beneath.

The leaves of the Narrow-Leaved Scribbly Gum are **lanceolate** in shape and range between 7-15 cm in length and 1-1.5 cm wide. They are a dull greyish green colour and often display a drooping arrangement.

Flowering usually occurs in winter and spring however this is considered highly variable, with the white flowers of this species recorded as also appearing in mid-late summer.

General notes: Scribbly Gums are easily recognised by the markings on its bark, which are made by the larvae of Scribbly Gum Moths (genus *Ogmograptis*).

The female moth lays her eggs below the outer layer of bark and when the larvae appear they begin to bore a tunnel into the tree. This tunnel is long, meandering and often contains loops and zig zags. At the end of the tunnel, the larvae turn around and make their way back through the tunnel they created.

In response to the tunneling, the tree produces scar tissue which the larvae use as a highly nutritious food source to help them rapidly mature. The scribbles are exposed when the outer layer of bark falls from the tree.

Pink Bloodwood
(*Corymbia intermedia*)

Identifying features: The Pink Bloodwood is a medium to large tree reaching up to 30 m in height. The canopy cover of this species is sparse, however can measure up to 10 m in width.

The bark of this species is corky and tessellated in texture; and grey or brown in colour. The **lanceolate**-shaped leaves are 10-15 cm long, 2-3 cm wide and dark green in colour. White or cream flowers appear throughout December to March, followed by gum nuts up to 2 cm long and 1.5 cm wide.

General notes: The common name of this species comes from the pink colour of its timber.

Pink Bloodwoods closely resemble Red Bloodwoods (*Corymbia gummifera*), with the larger gumnuts and seeds of the Red Bloodwood the primary distinguishing feature.

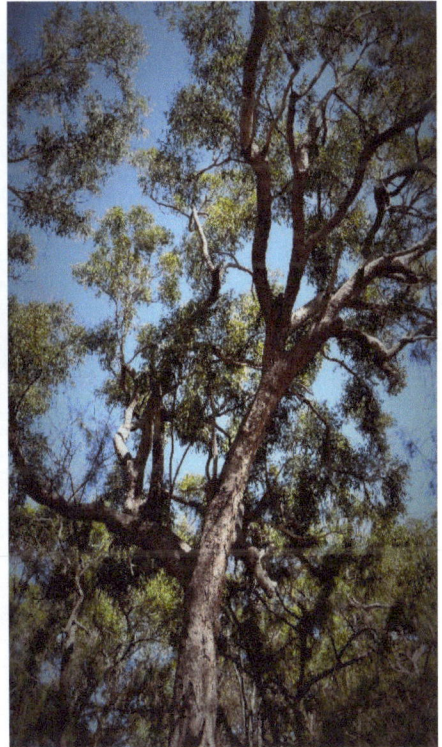

Queensland Blue Gum
(*Eucalyptus tereticornis*)

Other names: Red Gum; Flooded Gum; Grey Gum

Identifying features: The Queensland Blue Gum is an **evergreen** tree which grows to a height of between 20-50 m tall, developing a girth of up to 2 m.

The trunk is straight and singular for over half of the height of the tree. Rough, grey bark sheds, giving way to the smooth, mottled light-coloured wood beneath.

The glossy, green leaves of this species are **lanceolate**-shaped, between 8-22 cm in length and 1-3 cm wide. Fluffy white flowers appear in winter and spring.

General notes: The Queensland Blue Gum range extends from the wet tropics region of north Queensland to the southern coasts of New South Wales.

On the mainland, this species is an important food source for koalas.

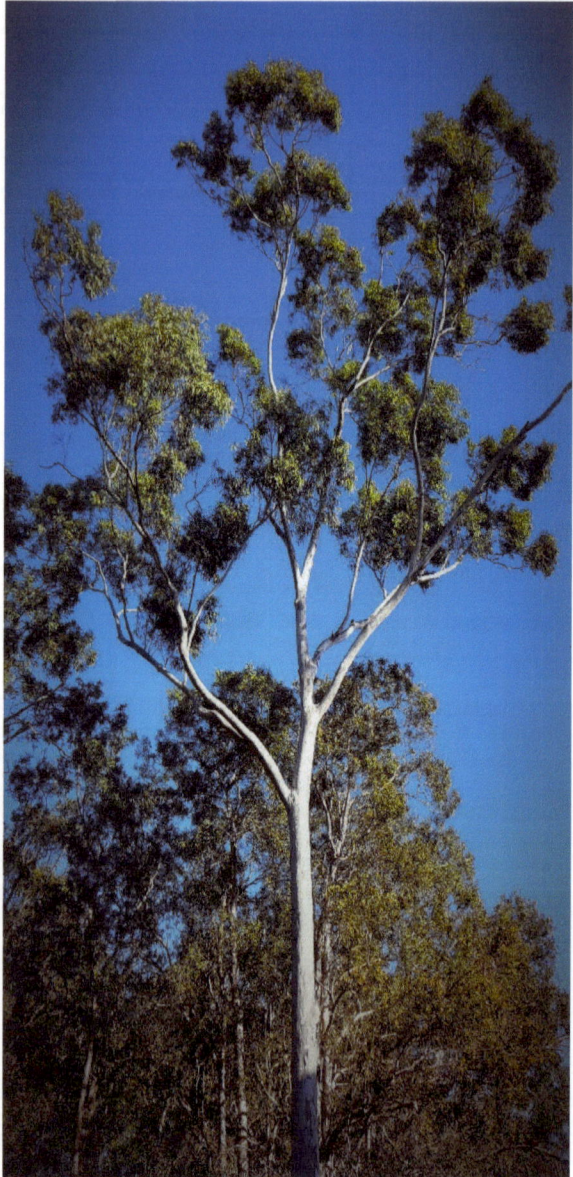

Smooth-Barked Apple
(*Angophora leiocarpa*)

Other names: Rusty Gum; Sugar Gum; Cabbage Gum

Identifying features: The Smooth-Barked Apple is a small to medium sized tree which grows to 25 m tall. The upper branches of this species are often bent and twisted. The outer layer of cream-grey bark sheds, revealing smooth orange-pink bark beneath.

The leaves of the Smooth-Barked Apple are glossy, green and **lanceolate**-shaped. Leaf length is between 5 and 16 cm, with a width of up to 2 cm. Flowering occurs in summer, when clusters of fluffy white flowers appear.

General notes: The Smooth-Barked Apple was originally classified as *Angophora costata* subsp. *leiocarpa*, however in 2000 it was re-classified and is now recognised as a species in its own right.

The scientific name '*Angophora*' is derived from the Greek words '*angos*', meaning 'a vessel' and '*phora*', meaning 'bearing' (which refer to the goblet-shaped seed capsules produced by this species). In addition, the Greek term '*leiocarpa*' means 'smooth' (*leio*) 'fruit' (*carpa*).

Swamp Mahogany
(*Eucalyptus robusta*)

Identifying features: The Swamp Mahogany is a tall tree which grows up to approximately 30 m in height. It is easily distinguished by its reddish-brown to grey-brown bark, which is rough, fibrous and deeply furrowed.

The leaves of this species are dark green and glossy, between 8.5-17 cm long and up to 7 cm wide. Flowering occurs between March and September, with peak flowering occurring throughout May and June. Flowers are white or cream and appear in clusters of between 7 and 13.

General notes: Swamp Mahogany provides habitat and food for many species, such as birds, bats, small mammals and insects.

The Swamp Mahogany has, reportedly, been utilised in folk medicine as a remedy for various ailments such as colds, flu, boils, abscesses, and dysentery, among others.

RAINFOREST

Rainforests are diverse ecological communities, housing an array of vegetative species such as trees, vines, ferns, **epiphytes** and shrubs. In addition, many animal species such as birds, mammals, reptiles and insects rely on rainforests for food and habitat.

Estimates suggest that rainforests cover only 10% of Earth, however they contain more than 50% of the world's total species (many of which are yet to be discovered).

The rainforest of Fraser Island (K'Gari) is classified as 'subtropical' and contains obvious vegetative layers. The understory includes a variety of low growing plants such as ferns; plus other species such as lichen, mosses and fungi. Many of the organisms found in this layer of the rainforest play a key role in the decomposition of dead and decaying plants and animals.

The mid layer of the rainforest provides habitat for a diverse range of animals, with many of the plant species found here producing fruit on their trunk rather than higher up in the canopy.

Canopy cover in rainforests is usually lush and dense, which prevents the majority of sunlight from filtering through to the forest floor.

As a result, much of the water transpired from the leaves of the plants is recirculated throughout the forest. This helps to regulate temperature and humidity.

Rainforests are incredibly important environments. They perform the 4 **ecosystem services** of cultural, supporting, provisioning and regulating, which provide multiple benefits for humans.

These services, however, depend upon healthy ecosystems, such as the rainforests found of Fraser Island (K'Gari) and the ongoing and complex functions they perform. Examples of the services provided by rainforests are:

Cultural – The services provided under this category are those which relate specifically to the scientific and intrinsic values of natural experiences within rainforests, such as recreational experiences; education and scientific research and Indigenous peoples spiritual and cultural connection to Country.

Provisional – Services within this category are those which supply valuable commodities such as fresh water, food, fuel, fibre and medicine.

Supporting – These include long-term processes which are fundamental to maintaining life support systems such as nutrient cycling, provision of habitat, production of oxygen, erosion prevention and flood mitigation.

Regulating – Regulating services are those relating to productivity, including climate regulation, carbon sequestration, seed dispersal and pollination.

Rainforests are often described as the lungs of the earth due to the significant role they play in converting carbon dioxide into oxygen. In addition, they function as sinks through the long-term storage of carbon. This helps to reduce atmospheric greenhouse gases, and is an important process for reducing the impacts of climate change.

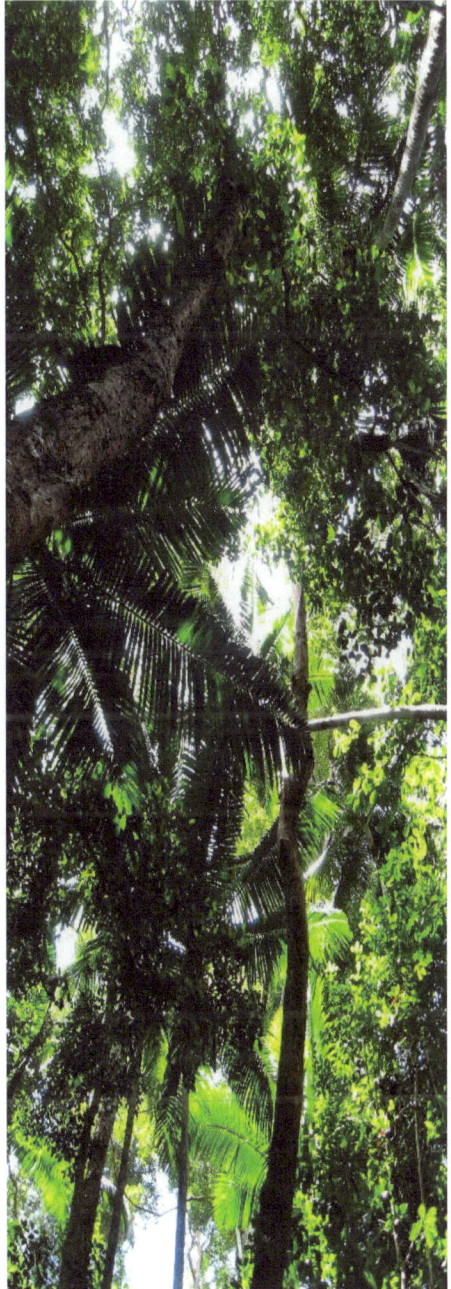

Blue Tongue
(*Melastoma affine*)

Other name: Native Lassiandra

Identifying features: The Blue Tongue is an **evergreen** shrub which reaches a height of 2 m. The deep green leaves of this species are **ovate** in shape and covered in fine hair. Three prominent veins run the length of the leaf.

Purple flowers appear in spring and summer, followed by the formation of gumnut-like fruits. When mature, the fruit will burst open to reveal the edible purple-coloured flesh contained inside.

General notes: The common name 'Blue Tongue' stems from the edible pulp, which stains the mouth blue. This pulp is very sweet, with a flavour similar to currents.

Blue Tongue flowers produce no nectar, however they provide large amounts of pollen for the native bees they rely on for reproduction.

Brush Box
(*Lophostemon confertus*)

Other names: Vinegartree; Pink Box; Box Scrub

Identifying features: The Brush Box is a medium sized tree which can grow up to 40 m high. It has a trunk diameter of 1-2 m, scale-like brown bark around the base of the tree and smooth, brownish-coloured bark on the remainder of the trunk and higher limbs.

The leaves of the Brush Box are dark green and leathery, ranging in size from 7-15 cm in length and 2.5-4.5 cm wide.

Clusters of cream-coloured, star-shaped flowers appear in spring and summer.

General notes: The leaves of the Brush Box are crowded at the ends of its branches. This gives rise to part of its scientific name, as '*confertus*' is Latin for 'crowded'.

This species was logged extensively on Fraser Island (K'Gari), with its timber used to produce bench tops, flooring, framing and croquet mallets. It was also used to construct marine piles.

Bush Cherry
(*Syzigium australe*)

Other names: Brush Cherry; Creek Lily Pilly

Identifying features: The Bush Cherry is a small to medium sized tree. It produces dark green, glossy leaves which are **lanceolate** in shape and up to 8 cm in length.

Fluffy white flowers appear in clusters during summer, followed by edible pinkish-coloured fruits measuring approximately 2 cm long.

General notes: This species occurs more commonly around creeks on Fraser Island (K'Gari).

The fruits produced by the Bush Cherry have a high water content, with a flavor similar to watermelon. It is often used to make lilly pilly jam.

Cinnamon Myrtle
(*Backhousia myrtifolia*)

Other names: Grey Myrtle; Silky Myrtle, Carrol, Ironwood

Identifying features: The Cinnamon Myrtle is a large shrub, reaching up to 7 m in height. The bark of this species is rough, scaly and greyish-brown in colour, becoming fissured with age.

It produces dense dark green foliage which are **lanceolate** in shape and between 4-7 cm long. Colouration of the leaves is darker on the upper surface. Fluffy white star-shaped flowers appear in spring and summer, which give way to small seed capsules attached to white **calyx** lobes.

General notes: When crushed, the leaves of this species give off a distinctive aroma similar to cinnamon, hence its common name.

The Cinnamon Myrtle is widely used as a spice in bush food cooking. It's leaves contain an essential oil called 'elemicin', which provides flavouring for various dishes including biscuits, curries or stews.

Common Silkpod
(*Parsonia straminea*)

Identifying features: The Common Silkpod is a long, woody climbing species which uses its **adventitious roots** to attach to its host plant.

The leaves of juvenile specimens differ to those of mature plants, in that juvenile leaves are soft, between 1-5 cm in length and display prominent venation on the dark green upper surface. Colouration of the lower surface is purple.

In contrast, mature leaves are **elliptic** to **oblong-ovate** in shape, leathery in texture, green on the upper surface and yellow on the lower surface. These leaves are also much larger (up to 24 cm long).

Clusters of small, hairy, 5-petaled flowers appear almost year-round, with colouration varying from pink to yellow.

Slender pods (up to 10 cm in length) then emerge. Each pod contains multiple seeds which are dispersed by wind when released.

General notes: The scientific name of this species, *Parsonia*, honours botanical author, James Parsons.

The Latin term *straminea* means 'straw-coloured', a possible reference to the feathery seeds.

Hairy Psychotria
(*Psychotria loniceroides*)

Other name: Mapoon Bush

Identifying features: The Hairy Psychotria is a shrub or small tree which can reach up to 5 m in height. The trunk of this species measures approximately 10 cm in diameter and is covered in smooth dark bark.

The leaves of the Hairy Psychotria measure between 6-10 cm and 1.5-5 cm wide, with a prominent **midrib** and veins. They also have a fine covering of soft hair. Colouration is mid to light green on the upper surface, while the lower surface is pale green. Leaf shape can vary between **ovate, elliptic** and **oblong**.

Clusters of white, 5-petaled tubular-shaped flowers appear between December and March, with the outside of the flower head covered in white hairs.

The creamy-yellow globular-shaped fruits which follow mature between February and September, measure up to 6 mm in diameter and contain a single oval-shaped seed.

General notes: This species is often found within the **ecotone** of rainforests and eucalypt forests, with its natural distribution ranging from south eastern New South Wales to far north Queensland.

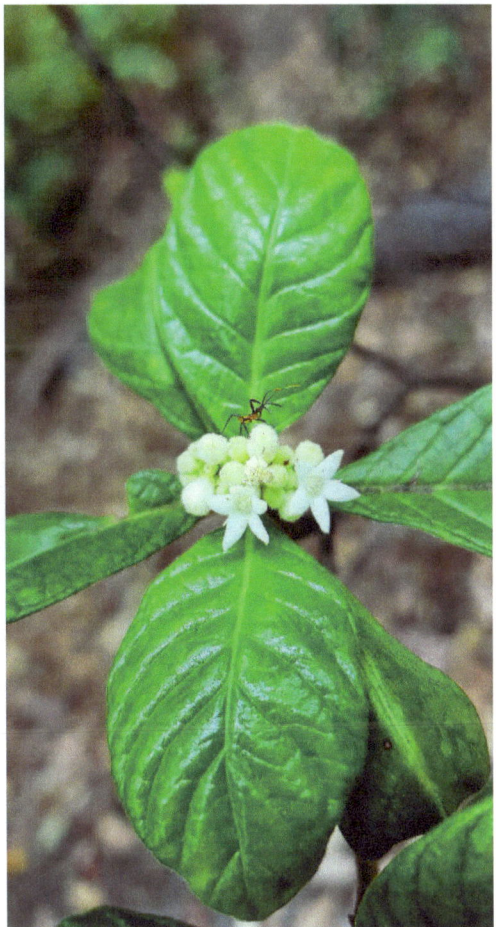

Hoop Pine
(*Araucaria cunninghamii*)

Identifying features: The Hoop Pine is a large, symmetrical-shaped tree, growing up to 60 m in height, with a trunk girth of 4 m. The bark of this species is rough and easily recognized by the scale-like horizontal hoops formed in the outer layer.

The leaves of Hoop Pines have a scaly texture, are fine, short and pointy and measure up to 2 cm long. Female seed capsules are egg-shaped, between 8-10 cm long and 6-8 cm wide; while male capsules are cylindrical (2-3 cm long; 5-7 mm wide).

General notes: The Hoop Pine is a **dioecious** species, with female seed capsules often appearing at the top of the tree. Female capsules usually appear at around 10 years, and approximately 22 years for males.

The scientific name of this species honours Botanist, Allan Cunningham, who collected and identified the first Hoop Pine specimen in the 1820s.

On Fraser Island (K'Gari), Hoop Pines were grown in plantations around Central Station. Their timber was considered valuable for furniture, plywood and panelling.

Kauri Pine
(*Agathis robusta*)

Identifying features: The Kauri Pine is a large **evergreen** tree growing between 30 to 50 m in height. The trunk of this species is tall and straight, measuring approximately 2 m in diameter. The bark of the Kauri Pine is grey-brown in colour, smooth and slightly flaky.

The leaves of Kauri Pines have a tough, leathery texture and are between 5-12 cm long and 1-4 cm wide. The upper surface is dark green and glossy, while the lower surface is pale. Fine veins run the length of each leaf blade.

Female seed capsules are egg-shaped, between 9-15 cm long and 8-10 cm wide; while the smaller male capsules are cylindrical (4-10 cm long; 7-15 mm wide). When mature, the capsules disintegrate to release the seeds contained within.

General notes: The Kauri Pine is **monoecious**, with both male and female seed capsules produced on the same plant (in different parts).

This species was heavily logged on Fraser Island (K'Gari), with its timber used for furniture, boat building, cabinetry and musical instruments.

King Fern
(*Angiopteris evecta*)

Other name: Giant Fern

Identifying features: The King Fern is an ancient (up to 300 million years old) **evergreen** species, which adopts the typical appearance of a fern. Its large **rhizome** forms a semi-woody trunk

It is the largest living fern in the world, growing up to 3 m in height and producing the longest fronds of any species (more than 5 m in length), which are bright green and arched.

General notes: On Fraser Island (K'Gari), approximately 30 individual plants grow alongside Wanggoolba Creek near the Central Station viewing platform, with a further 10 located upstream.

Typically, ferns are able to reproduce through the production of spores. However, due to climate and habitat restrictions, Fraser Island (K'Gari) King Ferns reproduce vegetatively by growing buds at the base of the fronds. These buds separate from the plant and establish themselves in the nearby substrate to produce a new plant.

Lemon Myrtle
(*Backhousia citriodora*)

Other name: Lemon Ironwood

Identifying features: Lemon Myrtle is an **evergreen** medium to large shrub, growing up to 8 m tall. The leaves of this species are glossy, bright green, **lanceolate**-shaped and 5-12 cm in length. A prominent **midrib** runs the length of the leaf.

Creamy-white flowers appear in clusters throughout summer and autumn. The small petals of the flowers are approximately 5 mm long, and surround numerous lengthy **stamens**.

Following flowering, nut-like capsules appear. These contain small seeds which are released when the capsule matures and falls from the tree.

General notes: The oil contained in the leaves of the Lemon Myrtle comprise 90% citral oil, with the remaining 10% lemon oil. When crushed, the leaves release a strong and distinct lemon aroma. As with Cinnamon Myrtle, Lemon Myrtle has been widely used in bush food cooking.

Native Gardenia
(*Atractocarpus fitzalanii*)

Other names: Brown Gardenia; Yellow Mangosteen

Identifying features: The Native Gardenia grows between 3-10 m in height. Its woody trunk is covered in smooth grey bark.

The leaves of this species are large (10-18 cm long, 3-5 cm wide), **obovate** to oval-shaped, glossy and dark green, with conspicuous yellowish veins and **midrib.**

Between September and November small white, star-shaped, fragrant flowers appear, followed by round or oval-shaped fruit (3-7 cm in diameter), which ripen between April and June. The fruit contains soft segmented flesh containing multiple small white seeds.

General notes: The fragrance of the flowers produced by this species is similar to that of the Common Gardenia (*Gardenia jasminoides*).

The fruit of the Native Gardenia is edible and may be eaten raw. It is a popular bush tucker food and is often used in desserts and salads.

Native Violet
(*Viola hederacea*)

Other name: Ivy-Leaf Violet

Identifying features: The Native Violet is an **evergreen perennial** ground cover. The dense, dark green leaves of this species are kidney-shaped and **toothed** on the outer margin. They grow between 1-3 cm wide on stems of between 2-6 cm.

The flowers produced by this species appear singularly on stalks up to 17 cm in height and are visible almost all year-round.

The petals are 7-10 mm in length and mauve and white in colour.

General Notes: The Native Violet is a widespread species. It is commonly found throughout Victoria New South Wales, Tasmania and South Australia.

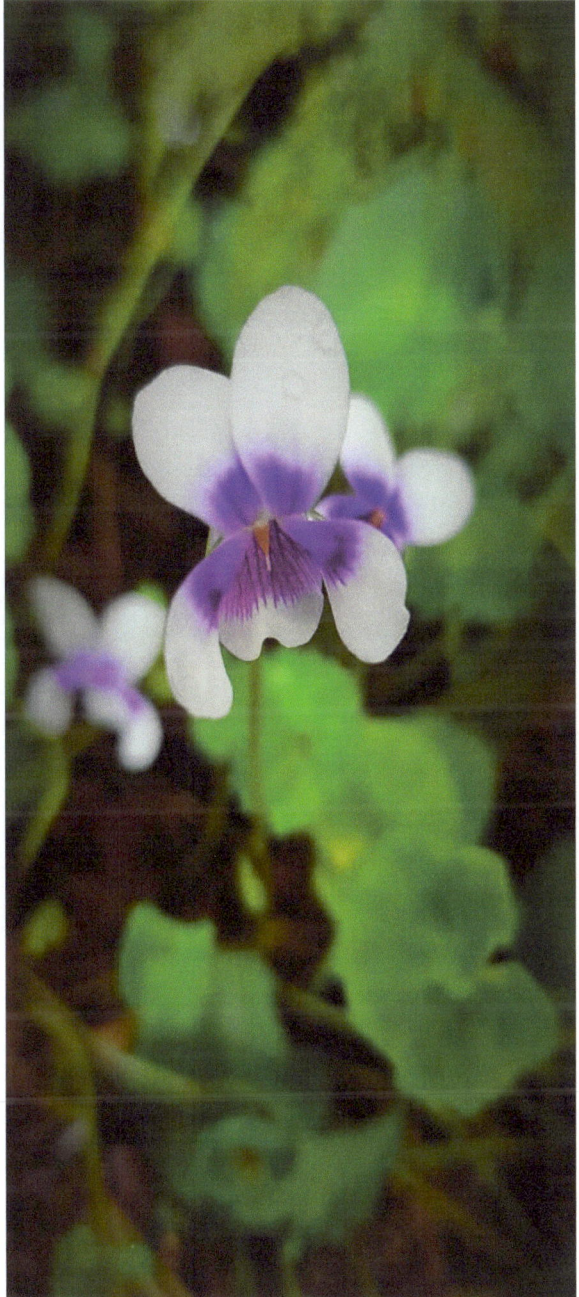

Picabeen Palm
(*Archontophoenix cunninghamiana*)

Other name: Bangalow Palm

Identifying features: The Picabeen Palm is a large species, growing up to 20 m in height, with a single straight and slender stem which is up to 30 cm in diameter.

The fronds of this species are glossy, dark green on the upper surface and lighter underneath, reaching up to approximately 4 m long. From afar, the numerous leaflets along each frond give it a feather-like appearance.

Small violet/lilac flowers appear on cream coloured stalks during summer, with round green fruit, up to 12 mm in diameter, following and becoming red as they mature.

General notes: Picabeen Palms grow tall and slender in order to break through the dense canopy of the rainforest to reach sunlight.

The Picabeen Palm is the only palm species located at Central Station.

The red fruit provides an important food source for many bird species.

The name 'Picabeen' derives from the Aboriginal use of the leaves as a water vessel ('pikki').

The scientific names of this species honours English Botanist and explorer, Allan Cunningham.

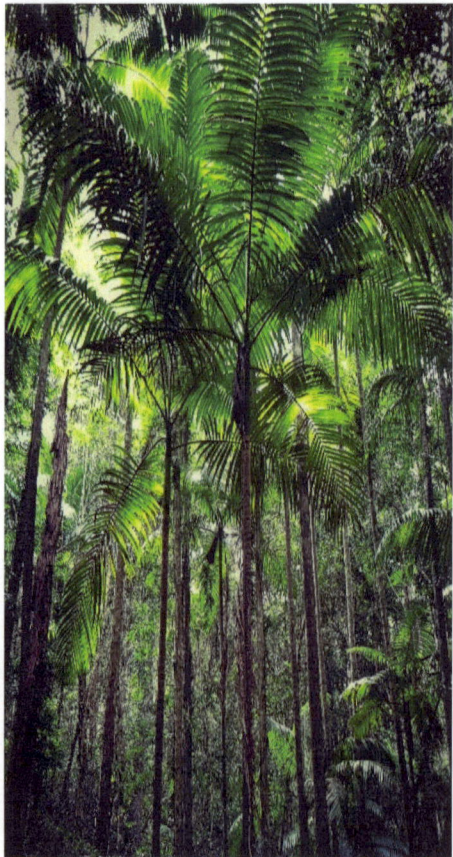

Red-Fruited Palm Lily
(*Cordyline rubra*)

Identifying features: The Red-Fruited Palm Lily is an **evergreen** shrub which grows to a maximum height of approximately 4 m. It produces glossy, green leaves which are between 15-50 cm in length, 3-6 cm wide and narrow **elliptic** in shape.

White to lilac-coloured flowers appear in summer, followed by numerous globular-shaped berries. The berries become red as they mature and measure approximately 1 cm in diameter.

General notes: The Red-fruited Palm Lily was first described in 1848 by German Botanists, Christoph Friedrich and Albert Gottfried Dietrich.

The scientific name of the Red-Fruited Palm Lily, '*Cordyline*', comes from the Greek word 'cordyle', meaning 'club'. This is thought to be in reference to the club-like appearance of some stems of this species. The word, '*rubra*', comes from the Latin 'ruber', meaning 'red', a reference to the colour of the berries.

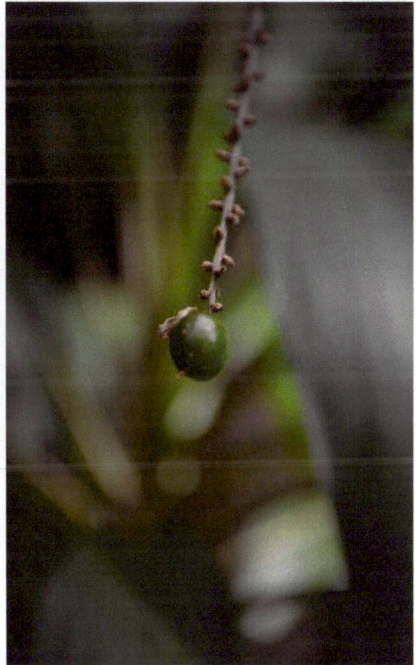

Satinay
(*Syncarpia hillii*)

Other names: Fraser Island Satinay; Fraser Island Turpentine

Identifying features: The Satinay is a medium sized **evergreen** tree which can attain a height up to 30 m. The trunk of this species can reach over 3 m in diameter, however the majority of Satinays of this size were removed from the island during the logging era. The trees that remain are approximately 1 m in diameter.

The bark of the Satinay is brown in colour, fibrous and heavily fissured, making it easy to identify. Satinay seed pods are similar to those produced by eucalypt species, however Satinay pods are fused together.

General notes: This species occurs mainly on Fraser Island (K'Gari), with great examples found at Pile Valley. Small plots of Satinay, however, are also found on the mainland, within the Cooloola region to the south.

Timber taken from Fraser Island (K'Gari) Satinays was used to construct the Suez Canal and to rebuild the London Docks after WWII.

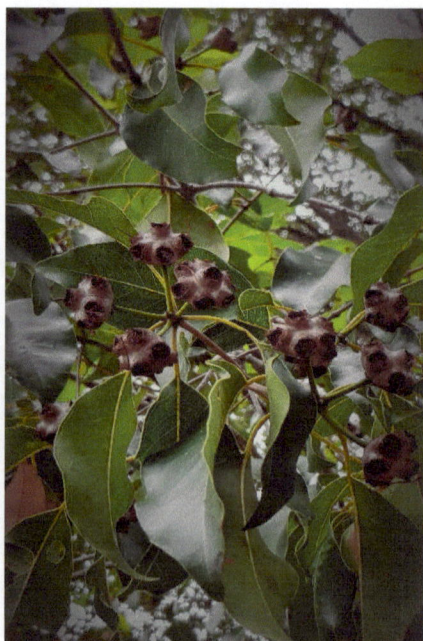

Staghorn Fern
(*Platycerium superbum*)

Identifying features: The Staghorn Fern is an **ephiphyte**, forming broad fronds, up to 60 cm in diameter. These fronds are sterile, with their primary function to embrace their host plant and create a bowl.

Fertile fronds hang down from the front of the plant. They can reach up to 2 m in length and measure approximately 2-6 cm wide. During summer these fronds produce a mass of spores on their underside.

General notes: This species gets its common name from the shape of its fronds (both fertile and infertile), which are broad and branching, resembling the antlers of a stag.

Staghorn Ferns feed on the detritus created by bark, flowers, leaves and water which are caught in the bowl created by their sterile fronds.

Like most **epiphytes** Staghorn Ferns generally grow high up on their hosts in order to take advantage of the increased availability of sunlight.

Strangler Fig
(*Ficus watkinsiana*)

Other names: Watkin's Fig; Green-Leaved Moreton Bay Fig

Identifying features: The Strangler Fig is a large **monoecious** tree which can grow up to 50 m in height. It is easily identified by the vine-like trunk surrounding its host tree.

The leaves of this species are between 5-21 cm in length and 2.5-9.5 cm wide. The fruit it produces is purple, rounded and up to 4 cm long.

General notes: Strangler Figs are **hemiepiphytes**, germinating from seeds deposited high up in the rainforest canopy by birds.

After germination the strangler fig sends roots down toward to the forest floor where it is able to access nutrients and to become more established.

Eventually the Strangler Fig completely surrounds its host tree, which inevitably dies as a result of being out competed for nutrients, or being unable to access the sunlight it needs for **photosynthesis**.

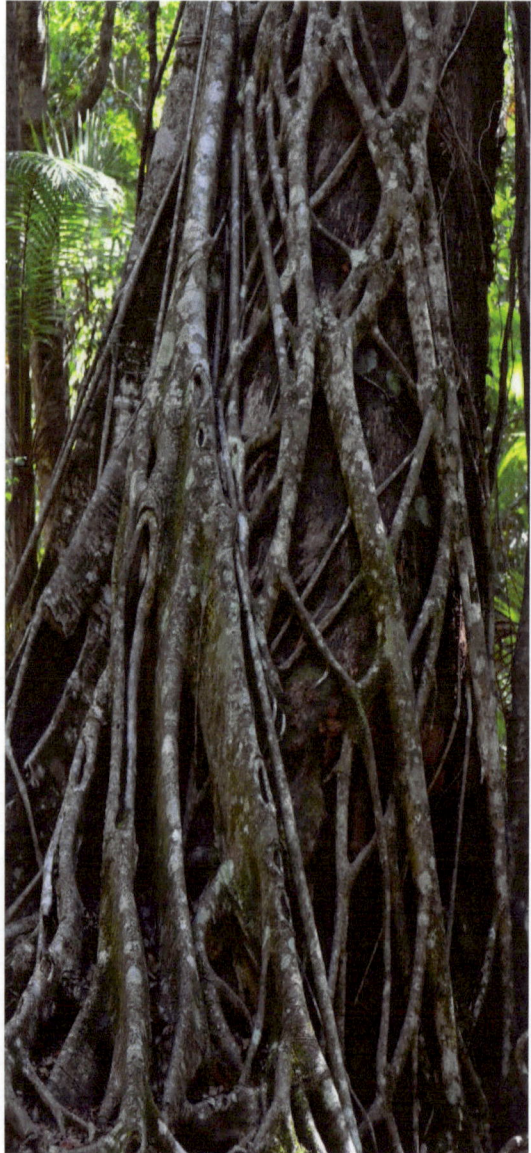

Swamp Lily
(*Crinum pedunculatum*)

Other names: Spider Lily; River Lily; Mangrove Lily

Identifying features: The Swamp Lily is a perennial bulbous herb with a tufted appearance. It can reach a height of up to 2 m, with a spread of between 2-3 m. The fleshy leaf blades of this species are bright green, between 1.3-1.5 m long and up to 15 cm wide. Multiple veins run the length of each leaf.

Flowering occurs from November to March, when clusters (10-25) of fragrant white flowers (10 cm in diameter) appear on tall thick stems up to 80 cm in height. The anther filaments (up to 6.5 cm long) vary between pink, red or purple in colour, with the anther itself either purple or black. Flowering is followed by the appearance of round capsules between 2-5 cm in diameter, which contain up to 9 irregularly shaped seeds.

General notes: The scientific '*Criunum*' derives from the Greek 'Crinon' (a lily), while '*pedunculatum*' comes from the Latin 'pedunculatus' ('with a peduncle'), a reference to the tall flower stems.

Tallow Wood
(*Eucalyptus microcorys*)

Identifying features: The Tallow Wood is a large tree which can grow up to 70 m, although on Fraser Island (K'Gari) it more often reaches between 40-50 m. Tallow Woods are easily identified due to their rough red-brown or brown-black bark, which is spongy and fibrous.

The leaves of the Tallow Wood are long, **lanceolate** to **ovate** in shape, between 6 and 15 cm long and 1.5 to 3.5 cm wide. Colouration is glossy green on the upper surface, with the lower surface more dull in appearance.

Tallow Woods produce a denser canopy than most eucalypts, therefore providing more shade.

Whiteish flowers appear at the end of branchlets, with flowering occurring in winter and spring.

General notes: The common name of this species is derived from the greasy feel of its timber when cut (ie. tallow = animal fat), which is used to make decking and outdoor furniture.

Tallow Woods are commonly seen around Central Station.

On the mainland, they are a primary source of koala food.

White Beech
(*Gmelina leichhardtii*)

Other name: Grey Teak

Identifying features: The White Beech is a medium sized tree which can reach heights of between 30–40 m. Older specimens of this species can often been found with **flanging** at the base. Bark colouration varies between light and dark grey, with the surface texture somewhat scaly. New shoots and older branchlets are covered in fine hairs.

The leaves of the White Beech measure between 8 and 20 cm in length and 5-10 cm wide, with a prominent **midrib** and veins. Colouration is dark green on the upper surface, while the lower surface is almost fawn. The lower surface also contains multiple fine hairs.

Clusters of tubular-shaped (20-25 mm long), creamy-white flowers with yellow and purple markings appear in spring and summer. These are followed by globular-shaped fruits up to 20 mm in diameter, which become blue-purple when ripe.

General notes: The White Beech is semi-**deciduous**, due to losing part of its canopy during spring.

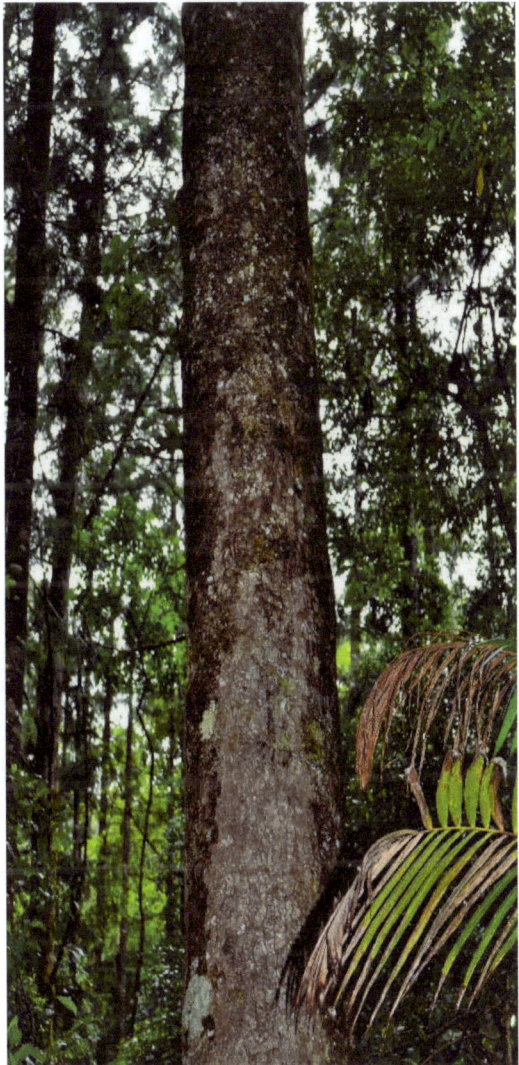

Zamia Palm
(*Macrozamia douglasii*)

Identifying features: Zamia Palms appear trunkless, with long, glossy, deep green fronds seemingly emerging directly from the ground. These fronds can grow up to 3.5 m in length, with individual plants producing between 30 and 100 each.

This species produces pineapple-like cones, measuring 10-60 cm in length, at the base of their fronds. These contain orange-coloured fruit that is often visible between the spiky outer layer of the cone.

General notes: Zamia Palms are an ancient species of plant which, although they appear similar to palms or ferns, belong to a primitive group called 'cycads'.

The fruit of Zamia Palms is toxic and should never be eaten raw. The Butchulla people of Fraser Island (K'Gari) undertook a labour intensive process to prepare a bread from them, a staple of their diet.

MIXED FOREST

The mixed forests of Fraser Island (K'Gari) provide habitat for a range of vegetative species, which often overlap with those found in other communities on the island. The plants found here are larger that those found within the coastal areas, yet not as tall as those within the tall eucalypt forests.

This is due to the nutrient layer beginning to develop here and becoming more readily accessible by resident plant species. Additionally, these plants are not subjected to the harshness of constant exposure to salt water and wind, which combined with increased nutrient access, allows trees to grow taller.

Many of the species found within the mixed forests consists of a variety of understory vegetation such as grasses, sedges and ferns. Medium sized shrubs are common and often produce striking flowers.

Larger trees provide ideal habitat for nesting birds and other species such as flying foxes and sugar gliders.

Black She-Oak
(*Allocasuarina littoralis*)

Identifying features: The Black She-Oak is an erect, **evergreen** tree which grows to approximately 10 m in height.

The dark grey/brown fissured bark of the trunk contrasts with the deep green of the fine branchlets which generally form upright needle-like structures.

She-Oaks are **dioecious**, with male plants producing showy red flower spikes throughout autumn and winter, often becoming yellow when full and covered with pollen. Female plants, in contrast, produce numerous cylindrical cones 1-3 cm in length.

General notes: All She-Oaks are **pioneering** nitrogen-fixing species. Microorganisms contained in the root system of these plants convert atmospheric nitrogen into a form more readily available to the plant. This enables other species, with higher nutrient requirements, to also establish.

The term '*Allocasuarina*' means 'the other Casuarina', while '*littoralis*' comes from Latin and means 'of, or coming from, the seashore'.

Blueberry Ash
(*Elaeocarpus reticulatus*)

Other name: Fairy Petticoats

Identifying features: The Blueberry Ash is a small, **evergreen** tree, reaching up to 15 m high, with a dense canopy spread of 3-5 m. The leathery, dark green leaves are **lanceolate**-shaped and turn bright red with age. They are up to 12 cm in length, between 1-3 cm wide and have prominent veins extending from the **midrib**. The bark of this species is brown and fissured.

Flowering occurs in summer, when masses of small white or pink bell-shaped and aniseed-scented flowers appear. Flowering is followed by the appearance of small, oval-shaped bright blue fruit, which are often retained on the plant throughout the year.

General notes: The fruit of this species contains a large seed, and is edible when it turns blue. While the fruit remains firm, however, it is **astringent**. As the fruit softens it develops a floury taste.

Bracken Fern
(*Pteridium esculentum*)

Other name: Austral Bracken

Identifying features: Bracken Ferns produce a long **rhizome**, between 2-10 mm in diameter and densely covered in fine red-brown hairs. The rhizome gives rise to stiff, upright, triangular-shaped fronds which grow between 0.3-2.5 m in length.

The leaves on the fronds are bright green and glossy. The upper surface of the leaves are darker in colour and typically smooth. The underside however, is often paler than that of the upper surface and covered in fine hairs and sporangium (see **sporangia**).

General notes: The scientific name of this species is taken from both the Greek and Latin words 'pteris' (Greek) meaning 'fern' and 'esculentum' (Latin) meaning 'food'.

The **rhizome** of the Bracken Fern was a staple in the diet of the Butchulla people and was eaten either raw or cooked (usually roasted).

Bungwall Fern
(*Blechnum indicum*)

Other name: Swamp Water Fern

Identifying features: Similar to Bracken Ferns, the tall, coarse fronds of Bungwall Ferns arise from a **rhizome**. As with Staghorn Ferns, however, Bungwalls produce both fertile and infertile fronds. These are similar in appearance, measuring up to 2 m in length.

The leaves on the fronds are **lanceolate**-shaped. New growth is pink-bronze in colour, maturing to a deep green. As with other fern species, the Bungwall Fern produces spores on the underside of the leaves on its fertile fronds.

General notes: The **rhizome** of the Bungwall Fern contains high levels of starch. It can be eaten either raw or cooked.

In 1770, Joseph Banks and Daniel Solander collected specimens of the Bungwall Fern from Botany Bay, along with another species of swamp fern, *Cyclosorus interruptus*.

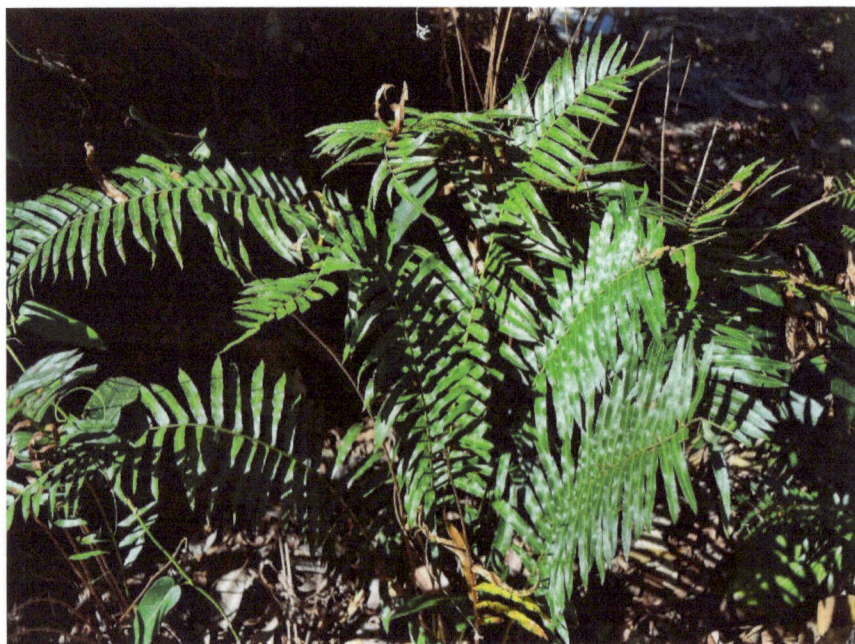

Bushy White Beard
(*Leucopogon margarodes*)

Other names: Pearl Beard Heath; Pink-Headed Heath

Identifying features: The Bushy White Beard is a spreading shrub growing up to 3 m in height. The stem of this species is typically reddish in colour and covered with small, fine, white hairs.

The leaves are up to 1.2 cm in length, with the widest part towards the upper end. The leaf margins are rounded underneath. Colouration is bright green on the upper surface and paler underneath. Venation is visible on the lower leaf surface.

Small, white, tubular-shaped flowers with a hairy throat appear all year, either singularly or in sparse groups of 2. The egg-shaped fruits produced by this species are green with a white fleshy base and is often sparsely covered in bristles.

General notes: The Bushy White Beard was first discovered in Australia by Scottish Botanist, Robert Brown, during the voyage of discovery undertaken by Matthew Flinders between 1801 and 1803.

Cypress Pine
(*Callitris columellaris*)

Other names: Coast Cypress Pine; White Cypress Pine

Identifying features: The Cypress Pine is a **monoecious** medium-sized tree with spreading branches, which attains heights of up to 30 m. The trunk is singular and erect, with rough and furrowed brown bark.

The leaves of this species are scale-like, 1-3 mm in length and appear on glossy, dark green branchlets in whorls of 3 (see **whorled leaves**). Both male and female cones can appear either solitary or in clusters. Male cones are cylindrical in shape, 3-10 mm long and 2 -5 mm wide. Female cones are larger, measuring 12-20 mm in diameter

General notes: When mature, the female cones of the Cypress Pine will fall from the tree, releasing the numerous, chestnut-brown winged seeds inside.

The scientific name, '*Callitris*', comes from the Greek words 'calli', meaning 'beautiful' and 'treis', meaning 'three' (referring to the leaves of this species).

Flax Lily
(*Dianella revoluta*)

Other names: Blueberry Lily; Blueberry Flax Lily; Black-Anther Flax Lily;

Identifying features: The Flax Lily is an **evergreen perennial** herb which produces long, rigid, linear leaves from its underground rhizome. This species grows to approximately 1 m high with a spread of up to 1.5 m. The bright green leaves of the Flax Lily vary between 15–85 cm in length, with widths typically 4-15 mm.

Flowering occurs in spring, when clusters of star-shaped flowers appear on stalks taller than the foliage of the plant itself. Each flower has 6 bright blue-purple coloured petals, with yellow filaments and black anthers.

Following flowering, green fruits appear, turning bright blue when mature. These fruits measure between 4-10 mm in diameter and contain 3-4 dark, glossy seeds.

General notes: The leaves of the Flax Lily were used for a variety of purposes by the Butchulla people, such as basket weaving.

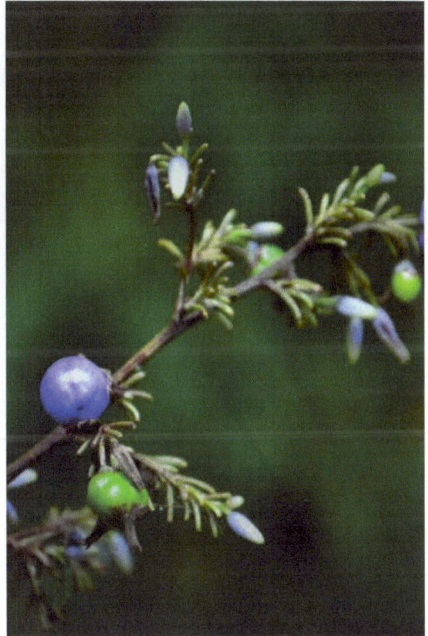

Forest Boronia
(*Boronia rosmarinifolia*)

Identifying features: The Forest Boronia is a small shrub reaching up to 2 m high.

The leaves of this species are long and narrow, with a rounded tip and a prominent **midrib**. The upper surface is glossy and deep green in colour, with the underside paler and rust-coloured. When crushed the leaves produce a strong aroma.

Flowering occurs throughout winter and spring, with the flowers of this species varying from pale to deep pink. Each flower contains 4 spreading petals which are between 7 and 9 mm long.

General notes: There are approximately 100 species of boronia occurring in Australia, which are commonly found on the sandy soils of dry open forests throughout Queensland and New South Wales.

The Forest Boronia belongs to the citrus family 'Rutaceae'.

Foxtail Sedge
(*Caustis blakei*)

Other names: Curleywigs; Koala Fern

Identifying features: The Foxtail Sedge is a tufting **perennial** which grows to a height of approximately 1.5 m. The fronds of this species are between 20-50 cm in length and sheathed by dark brown scale-like leaves. There are both fertile and infertile fronds.

The hairy, soft, lime green branchlets which appear on the fronds make this species easy to identify. The branchlets of older fronds turn reddish-brown when mature and resemble the tail of a fox, giving rise to the common name 'Foxtail Sedge'.

Tiny brown flower spikelets, 6-7 mm in length, appear on the end of long, smooth, erect, stems. The fruit produced by this species is 4-6 mm long, up to 3 mm wide and straw-coloured.

General notes: Foxtail Sedges have a **symbiotic** relationship with an underground fungus, which grows on its root system. The fungus, essentially, extends the area of the root system and gives the plant better access to the nutrients it requires for survival.

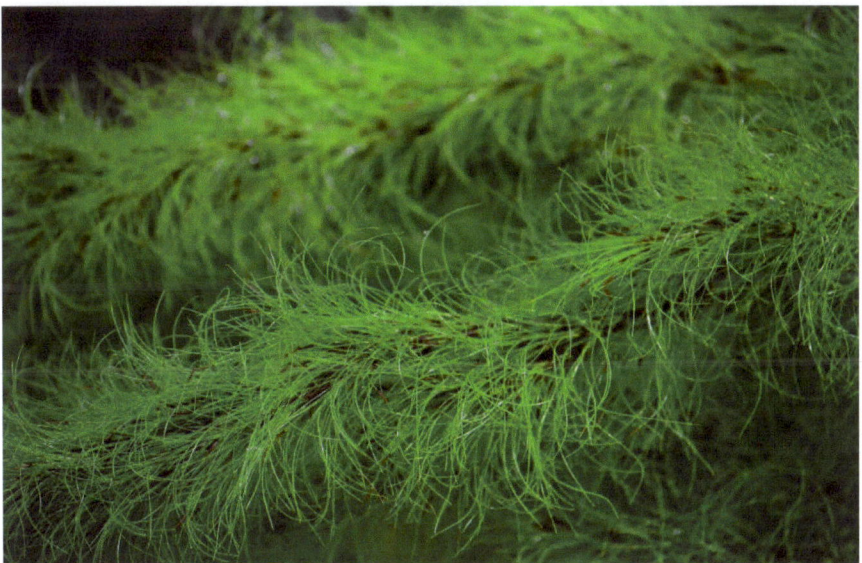

Heath Platysace
(*Platysace lanceolata*)

Identifying features: The Heath Platysace is a shrub which can grow up to 1.5 m in height. The stems of this species are often covered in fine hairs.

The bright green leaves appear alternately on the stems and measure between 1-5 cm in length and up to 15 mm wide. Leaf shape can vary, however is commonly **lanceolate** to **elliptic**. When crushed, the leaves produce a scent similar to that of carrots.

Between September and April masses of cream/white star-shaped flowers appear at the end of branches. Each flower produces 5 petals and measures between 1-3 mm in diameter.

Prior to opening, flower buds are often pink/red in colour. The warty fruit which follows is 1.5-2 mm long and 1.5-2.1 mm wide.

General notes: The first part of the scientific name, '*Platysace*' (Greek) means 'flat shield', a reference to its fruit.

The second part of the name comes from the Latin 'lancea' ('spear') and 'atus' ('like') a reference to the shape of the leaves of this species.

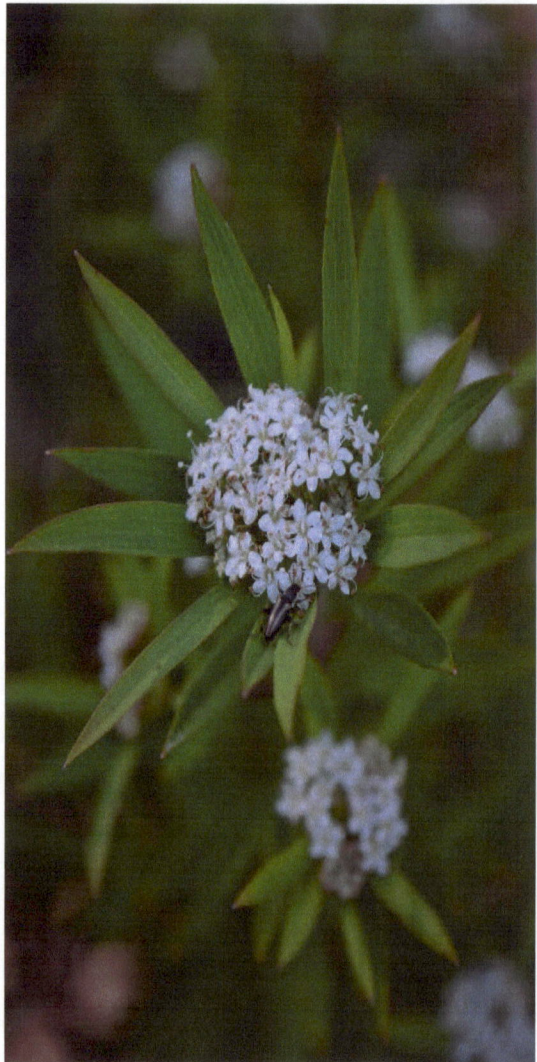

Hop Bush
(*Dodonaea triquetra*)

Identifying features: The Hop Bush is a small, erect, **dioecious** shrub between 2-3 m in height, with a spread of approximately 1.5 m. It produces soft, glossy, dark green, **elliptic**-shaped leaves up to 12 cm long and 1-5 cm wide.

The clusters of small, yellow-green flowers produced between June and October lack petals and do not produce pollinator-attracting nectar. As a result, the hop bush relies on wind for pollen distribution.

The fruit of this species resembles glossy 3-winged capsules, with each wing up to 16 mm in height and between 2-5 mm wide. When mature, the green capsules turn brown or purple, become dry/papery in texture and split to release the brown seeds inside.

General notes: The scientific name of the Hop Bush comes from the Latin '*Dodonaea*', after the 16th Century Botanist Rembert Dodoens; and '*triquetra*', meaning 'triangular', which refers to the 3-winged fruit capsule produced by this species.

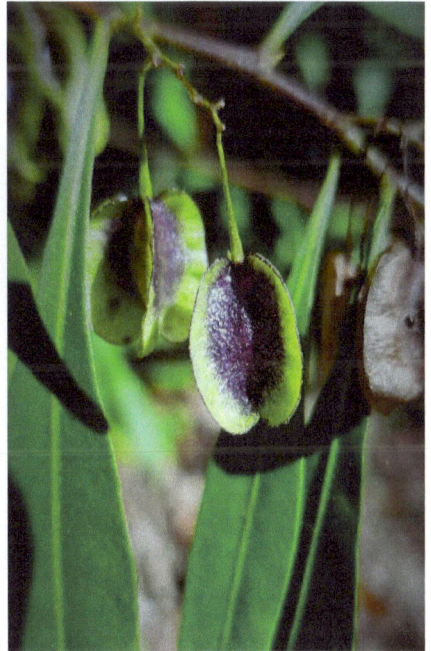

Johnson's Grasstree
(*Xanthorrhoea johnsonii*)

Other name: Forest Grasstree; Wallum Grasstree

Identifying features: Johnson's Grasstree is a small to medium herbaceous **perennial** shrub. Its distinct trunk grows up to 5 m in height. The spreading tufted crown of this species consists of bright green grass-like leaves 1-3 mm in width. Older leaves, however, hang downwards.

Flowering occurs from autumn to summer when flower spikes (up to 1.25 m long) bearing small white flowers appear on top of stems between 0.75 and 1.9 m in length and between 7-20 mm in diameter. Following flowering, multiple seed capsules appear along the flower spike, releasing small black seeds when mature.

General notes: Johnson's Grasstree is very slow growing, with reports suggesting it grows approximately 2-3 cm per year.

The name of this species honours Australian Botanist L.A.S. Johnson.

Midyim Berry
(*Austromyrtus dulcis*)

Other name: Midgen Berry

Identifying features: Midyim Berry is a spreading shrub which grows up to 1 m in height. The coarse leaves of this species are glossy, **lanceolate** to **elliptical** in shape, 3 cm long and up to 1 cm wide. The vibrant red of new growth becomes bright green as it matures, with colouration of the upper surface darker than that of the lower surface.

Small white flowers, which appear from spring through to autumn, are followed by white dark-speckled berries up to 6 mm in diameter.

General notes: The sweet and aromatic fruit of the Midyim Berry is able to be eaten straight off the plant. Considered a leisure food, due to the lack of preparation required to eat them, Midyim Berries are a popular bushfood eaten by the Butchulla People of the Island.

Midyim Berries can be seen growing all over Fraser Island (K'Gari).

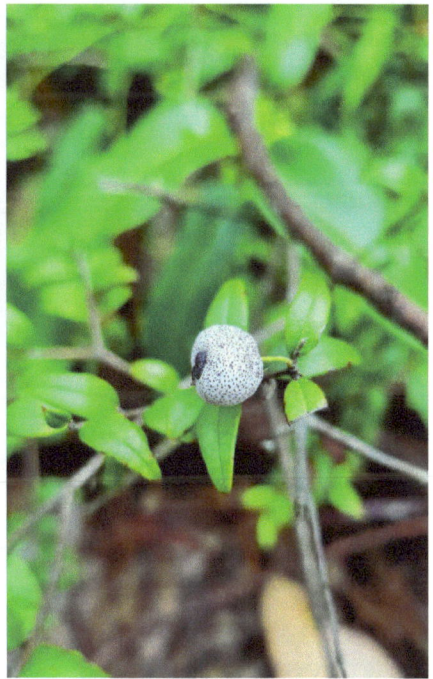

Mistletoe
(*Amyema sp.*)

Identifying features: The term 'Mistletoe' refers to a large group of **hemiparasitic** plants which attach themselves to a host tree in order to extract the nutrients and water they require to survive.

Within Australia, there are 85 different species of Mistletoe which are often found on Eucalypts, Acacias and Casuarinas. Most species of Mistletoe are host-specific, often mimicking the foliage of the species they grow in.

General notes: Mistletoe Birds are known to feed almost exclusively on the fruit of Mistletoe plants. They are also responsible for the spread of its seeds, which pass through the birds digestive system and deposited on a branch during defecation.

Many species of Mistletoe damage their host plant by reducing the growth of its branches, which results in stunted growth. Host plants which are heavily infested may die due to increased stress.

As well as birds, Mistletoe provides food for possums and sugar gliders.

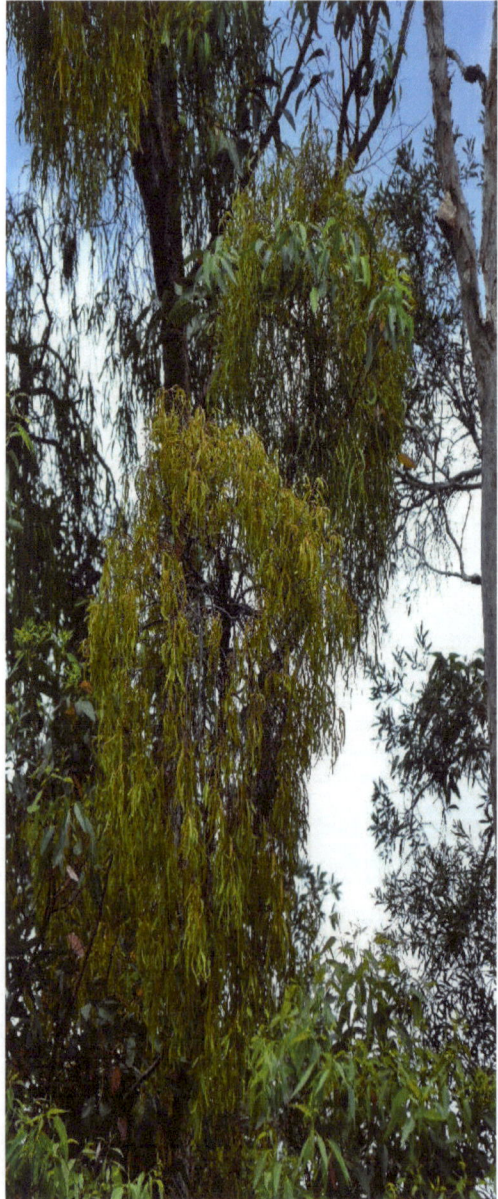

Narrow-Leaf Platysace
(*Platysace linearifolia*)

Other name: Carrot Tops

Identifying features: Narrow-Leaf Platysace is a shrub which reaches up to 1 m in height. The soft, narrow, linear leaves of this species are between 10-25 mm in length, with a width of 1 mm. When crushed, they emit a scent similar to carrots.

Between January and May small white, star-shaped flowers appear on slender erect stems. The fruit produced by this species are approximately 2 mm in length and width.

General notes: The scientific name of the Narrow-Leaf Platysace comes from the Greek '*Platysace*', meaning 'flat shield' as reference to the shape of the fruit. The Latin words '*linearis*' and '*folius*' (meaning 'line' and 'leaf', respectively) are combined to form '*linearifolia*', in reference to the linear-shaped leaves of this species.

Prickly Broom Heath
(*Monotoca scoparia*)

Identifying features: The Prickly Broom Heath is a **dioecious** shrub reaching up to 2.5 m in height. It also produces a spread of approximately 1.2 m.

The leaves of this species are narrow, **oblong-elliptic** in shape, between 6 and 15 mm long and 1-2 mm in width. Colouration of the upper surface is dark green, with the lower surface pale green to white.

Creamy-white tubular flowers appear in clusters of 2-9 during February and July, with peak flowering occurring throughout April and May. At 4 mm in length, male flowers are larger than females, which measure up to 2.6 mm.

The Prickly Broom Heath produces egg-shaped, fleshy, fruit up to 3 mm in length, which turn light yellow when mature.

General notes: This species will regenerate from a **lignotuber**.

Prickly Moses
(*Acacia ulicifolia*)

Other name: Juniper Wattle

Identifying features: The Prickly Moses is a small erect shrub of straggly appearance which reaches between 1–3 m in height. It's leaf-like **phyllodes** are between 10-12 mm long, approximately 1.5 mm wide and are sharply pointed. The **midrib** is raised on both the upper and lower surfaces.

Flowering mainly occurs in winter and spring, with the globular-shaped flowers white and yellow, or cream and yellow, in appearance.

The fruit produced by this species are between 2-6 cm long, 4-6 mm in width and dark brown-black in colour.

The seeds contained within are **oblong-elliptic** in shape and 3-5 mm in length.

General notes: The first part of the scientific name, '*Acacia*', comes from the Greek '*akakia*' and refers to the sharp **phyllodes**.

The second part of the name, *ulicifolia*, also refers to the foliage, and its similarity to that of the plant genus *Ulex* (which is more commonly known as Gorse).

Primrose Ball Wattle
(*Acacia flavescens*)

Other name: Toothed Wattle; Red Wattle; Yellow Wattle

Identifying features: The Primrose Ball Wattle is an **evergreen** tree which can reach heights of between 6 and 20 m. The trunk of this species is covered in layers of rough, furrowed bark, while the branchlets are often tinged yellow.

The leaf-like **phyllodes** are between 9 and 24 cm in length, 2-4 cm wide and narrowly **elliptic** to **lanceolate** in shape. Three prominent veins run the length of each.

Flowering occurs in autumn and winter with the appearance of cream globular-shaped flowerheads between 4.5 to 6 mm in diameter.

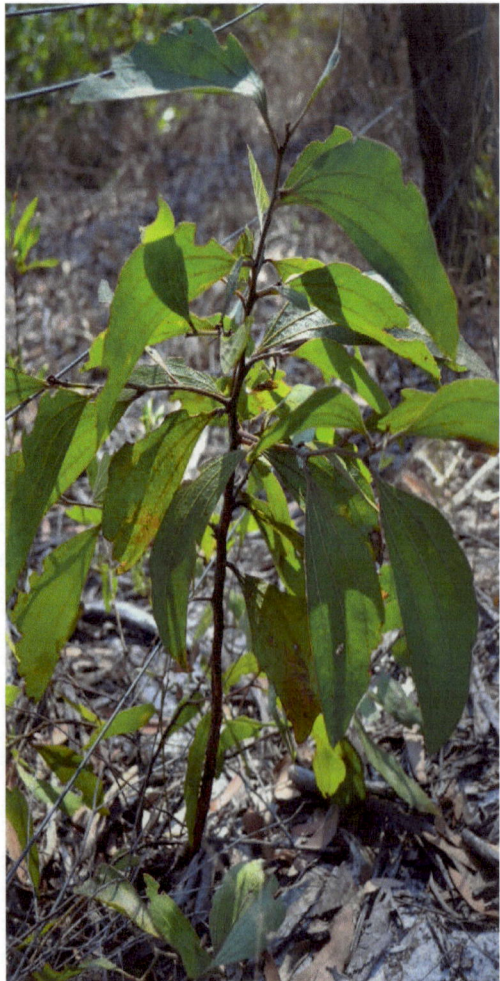

The seed pods which follow are flat, up to 12 cm in length and 2 cm wide. The seeds contained within are brown-black in colour, **elliptic** in shape and 7 mm long.

General notes: The first part of the scientific name, '*Acacia*', comes from the Greek '*akakia*' and refers to the sharp **phyllodes**.

The second part of the name '*flavus*' comes from the Latin (meaning 'yellow') and is a reference to the branchlets.

Showy Guinea Flower
(*Hibbertia linearis*)

Other name: Guinea Flower

Identifying features: The Showy Guinea Flower is an attractive species which can grow as either a small, erect shrub up to 2 m in height, or a diffuse spreading bush up to 60 cm tall. Younger stems are often covered in fine, sparse hairs which reduce and disappear as the stem ages.

The bright green leaves are **alternate** and often hairy on the lower surface. They are **linear-oblong** to **obovate** in shape, 8-30 mm long and 1-5 mm wide, with tips varying between rounded or pointy.

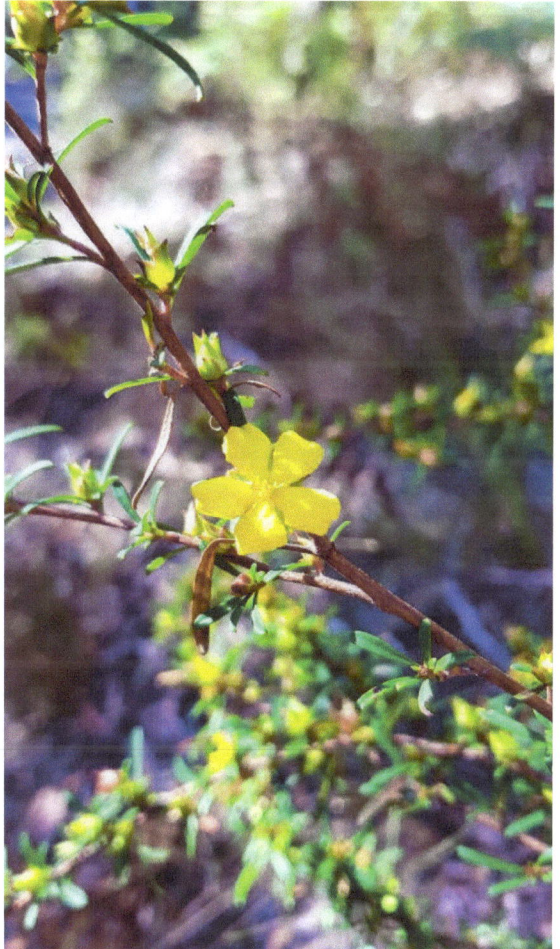

Flowering mainly occurs in spring and summer, when large bright 5-petaled yellow flowers appear.

The flowers measure up to 20 mm in diameter, with each petal between 8-10 mm in length. At the centre of each flower are 3 **carpels**, surrounded by 15-25 **stamens**.

General notes: The scientific name of this species honours British Botanist George Hibbit (*Hibbertia*). The Latin '*linearis*' means 'linear', a reference to the narrow, parallel-sided leaves.

Sickle Wattle
(*Acacia falcata*)

Other name: Sickle-Shaped Acacia; Hickory Wattle; Silver-Leaved Wattle

Identifying features: The Sickle Wattle is a **perennial** shrub or tree. It can reach heights of between 2 and 5 m and has an appearance which can vary between erect or spreading. The trunk of this species is slender and covered in grey or black bark.

The leaf-like **phyllodes** are sickle-shaped, measuring up to approximately 15 cm in length and between 9-30 mm wide. Colouration is usually grey-green, with a prominent **midrib** running the length of each **phyllode**.

Clusters of small, round creamy flowers appear between April and August, followed by thin seed pods up to 12 cm long. When mature, the pods release multiple shiny black seeds between 3.5-4.5 mm in length.

General notes: The Sickle Wattle gets its common name from the shape of its **phyllodes**.

This species is hardy and adaptable. It is useful for projects involving bushland regeneration within its native areas of Qld and NSW.

Slender Rice Flower
(*Pimelea linifolia*)

Other name: Rice Paper Plant; Queen of the Bush

Identifying features: The Slender Rice Flower is a small, erect shrub which grows between 1-1.5 m in height. The leaves are 4-30 mm long and 2-9 mm wide, with a prominent **midrib**.

Clusters of up to 60 white or pink, tubular-shaped flowers (1-2 cm long) occur at the end of branches during spring and summer, with the pollen produced bright orange in colour.

The fruit which follows is green, oval-shaped and between 3-5 mm long.

General notes: The Slender Rice Flower is commonly found through all states of Australia, with the exception of Western Australia and the Northern Territory.

This species provides critical food and habitat for many species, which includes ground parrots and butterflies. However it is considered toxic to livestock.

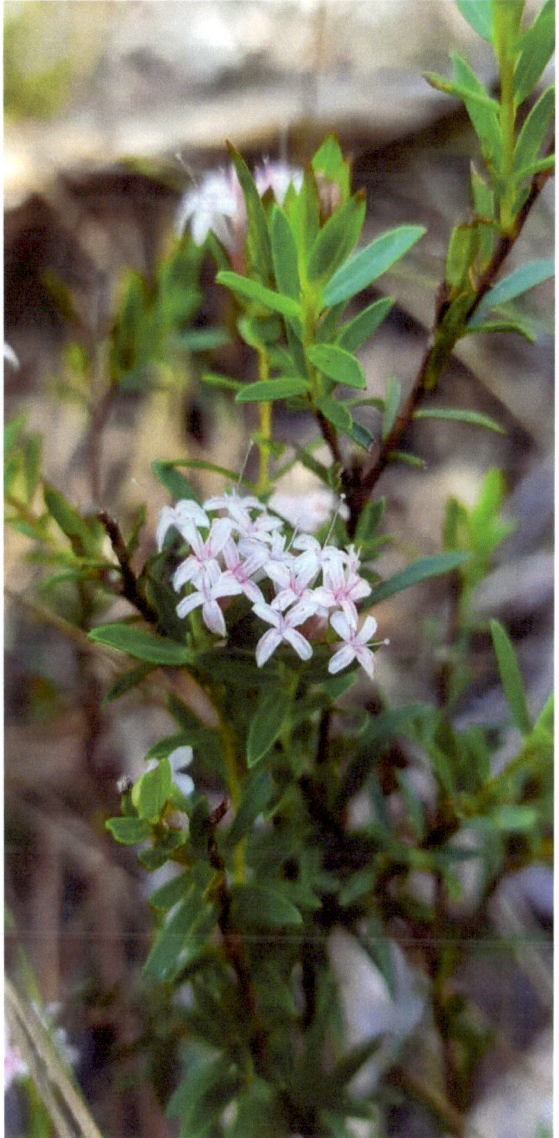

Spotted Hyacinth Orchid
(*Dipodium variegatum*)

Other name: Blotched Hyacinth Orchid; Slender Hyacinth Orchid

Identifying features: The Spotted Hyacinth Orchid is a leafless **saprophyte** which produces a green fleshy stem between 15-80 cm in height.

A small leaf usually occurs near the base of the plant.

Between 2 and 50 flowers, 11-15 mm long and 3-5 mm wide appear on the fleshy stem.

Colouration of the flowers is pale pink with purple splotches. The petals often turn slightly backwards.

General notes: Due to its distinct lack of leaves, the Spotted Hyacinth Orchid does not **photosynthesise**. Instead, its **symbiotic** relationship with an underground fungus provides it with the nutrients it requires to survive.

This species relies on native bees and wasps for pollination and reproduction.

Photo credit Ruth Thomas

Woombye
(*Phebalium woombye*)

Identifying features: The Woombye is a spreading shrub which grows to approximately 2 m in height and 1.5 m in width. The leaves of this species are **elliptic** in shape, ranging from **oblong** to broad, between 20 and 60 mm long and up to 10 mm wide. The upper surface of the leaves are dark green in colour, contrasting the lower surface which is silver.

Clusters of creamy-white, 5-petaled flowers appear in winter and spring, with each petal measuring up to 6 mm in length. The prominent yellow **stamens** slant to one side.

General notes: The leaves of this species are aromatic when crushed.

The first part of its scientific name comes from the Greek word, *'phebalios'*, a term for 'fig'.

There is uncertainty surrounding the source of the second part of its name, although this could perhaps refer to the town of Woombye, where it possibly may have been first recorded.

The nectar produced by the flowers of this species attracts White-Cheeked Honeyeaters.

WALLUM

Much of the coastal lowlands of south-east Queensland through to north-eastern New South Wales contains vegetative communities known as Wallum. This term is derived from an aboriginal name for the Wallum Banksia (*Banksia aemula*), however is now used to describe a specific type of ecosystem, in which Banksias feature prominently.

Wallum is generally characterised by swampy plains and nutrient deficient, acidic (pH 3.5 to 4.5) sandy soils. Within the Wallum areas of Fraser Island (K'Gari), window lakes are often featured, one of 3 types of lake found on the island. These occur when the level of the water table increases above the surface of the ground and becomes exposed. Despite the harshness of the Wallum environment it is a highly productive community, supporting a diverse array of plant-life well adapted for living here.

There are no large trees in Wallum, with most plants producing low, shrubby vegetation. This is due to low nutrient availability, particularly that of nitrogen and phosphorous. In response, competition for nutrients is high. Some species have overcome this, however, by developing symbiotic (see **symbiosis**) relationships with other organisms, such as fungi, to increase their access to nutrients.

Many Wallum species are fire-adapted, such as Banskias and Grasstrees. Fire is an important element for stimulating seed dispersal and germination within this ecosystem and is a regular occurrence here.

Wallum is an important and incredibly valuable ecosystem. It provides habitat for a multitude of plants and animals, many of which are unique to this community.

The large flowers and abundant nectar produced by Wallum species provides an important source of food for many animals, including honeyeaters, insects and mammals. As a result, birds can often be seen in the Wallum, with ground-dwelling as well as tree-dwelling species common.

In addition to food, Wallum supports a multitude of animal species by providing them with shelter. Marsupial mice, bandicoots, sugar gliders, skinks, snakes and flying foxes are all often found in Wallum areas.

In particular, Wallum provides important habitat for acid frogs such as the Wallum Froglet (*Crinia tinnula*), Wallum Rocket Frog (*Litoria freycinet*), Wallum Sedge Frog (*Litoria olongburensis*) and Wallum Tree Frog (*Litoria cooloolensis*), which are the only frog species able to survive in such acidic conditions.

From winter through spring the Wallum areas of Fraser Island (K'Gari) become a mass of colour, with the multitude of wildflowers found in these areas coming into bloom and creating an amazing visual display.

Although the Wallum found on Fraser Island (K'Gari) is protected, those found on the mainland face many threats. This includes development. Human populations are higher along coastal zones, where Wallum areas occur and many have already been lost.

Broad-Leaved Paperbark
(*Melaleuca quinquenervia*)

Other name: Paperbark Tea Tree; Fine-Veined Paperbark

Identifying features: The Broad-Leaved Paperbark is a small-medium sized tree, growing up to a height of 25 m. The most distinguishing feature of this species, however, is its bark, which consists of many beige, white and light grey paper-like layers.

The leaves of the Broad-Leaved Paperbark are a dull grey-green, between 5-12 cm long and 1-3 cm wide, with 5 parallel veins running from the base to the tip. The bottlebrush-like flowers are creamy white in colour and appear on the ends of branches between September and March.

General notes: Broad-Leaved Paperbarks are commonly the dominant species in swamps and floodplains. On Fraser Island (K'Gari) this species can be found growing within the coastal margins on both the eastern and western sides of the island.

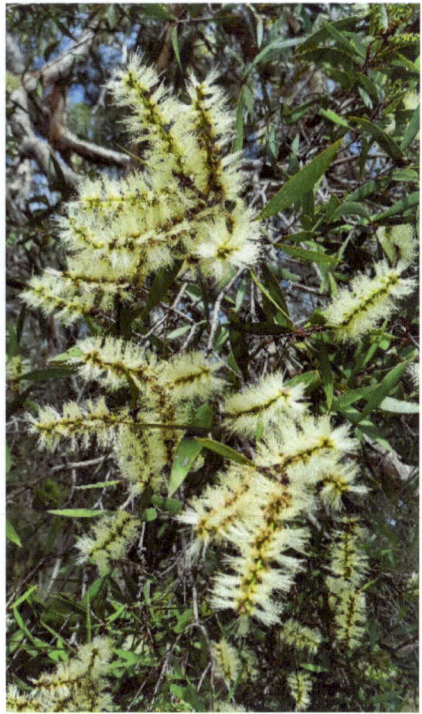

Cape Blue Water Lily
(*Nymphaea caerulea*)

Other name: Cape Water Lily; Blue Lotus; Blue Egyptian Lotus

Identifying features: The Cape Blue Water Lily is an aquatic **perennial** species. The floating broad, round, leaves it produces are approximately 30-40 cm in diameter and notched at the point of the stem which anchors it to the soil. The margins of the leaves are irregularly serrated.

Large light blue or mauve-coloured flowers (10-15 cm in diameter) occur on stems and sit up to 30 cm above the surface of the water. The centre of the flower, including the **stamens**, appear yellow however the tips of the **stamens** mimic the colour of the flowers petals.

General notes: The Cape Blue Water Lily is an introduced species. It is considered an environmental weed throughout Queensland due to its displacement of native species.

It is often confused with the native Giant Blue Water Lily (*Nymphaea gigantea*), which is not present on Fraser Island (K'Gari), however is thought to be almost extinct within South East Queensland.

Common Aotus
(*Aotus ericoides*)

Other name: Eggs and Bacon

Identifying features: The Common Aotus is a shrub which can grow up to 2 m in height. The branches and stems of this species are usually covered with a fine layer of fine silvery-coloured hairs.

The glossy, dark green leaves are between 6 and 20 mm long, 1-5 mm wide with slightly curved margins. They also often appear to have warty-like projections on their upper surface.

Flowering occurs in winter and spring, when clusters of bright yellow pea-shaped flowers with reddish-orange banding appear. This is followed by velvety, egg-shaped pods (6-7 mm long) containing 2 small black seeds which are released when mature.

General notes: Typically, pea flowers consist of 5 petals: the large upper petal (the 'standard'), 2 side petals ('wings') and 2 lower petals fused together ('keel'). The keel encloses the stigma and stamens.

Dodder Vine
(*Cassytha filiformis*)

Other name: Dodder Laurel; Devil's Twine; Love Vine

Identifying features: Dodder Vine is a twining parasitic vine. It's multiple green-orange stems reach up to 2 cm in diameter and between 3–8 m in length, with new shoot growth often covered in reddish-coloured hairs. The leaves of this species are scale-like and approximately 1 mm long.

Flowering can occur all year, with small flowers (2.5 mm diameter) appearing either singularly or in **spikes** between 2 and 2.5 cm long. The globular-shaped fruit which follows turns green when mature, measures between 4-10 mm in diameter and contains seeds 3-6 m in diameter.

General notes: Dodder Vines attach to their host plant/s using their 1-2 mm long **haustoria**.

This species is considered both partially and completely **parasitic**. Young green-coloured growth contains **chlorophyll**, allowing the plant to **photosynthesise**. As the plant ages and stems darken to orange-red, it can no longer **photosynthesise** due to the absence of the **chlorophyll**. The plant is then entirely dependent upon its host for survival.

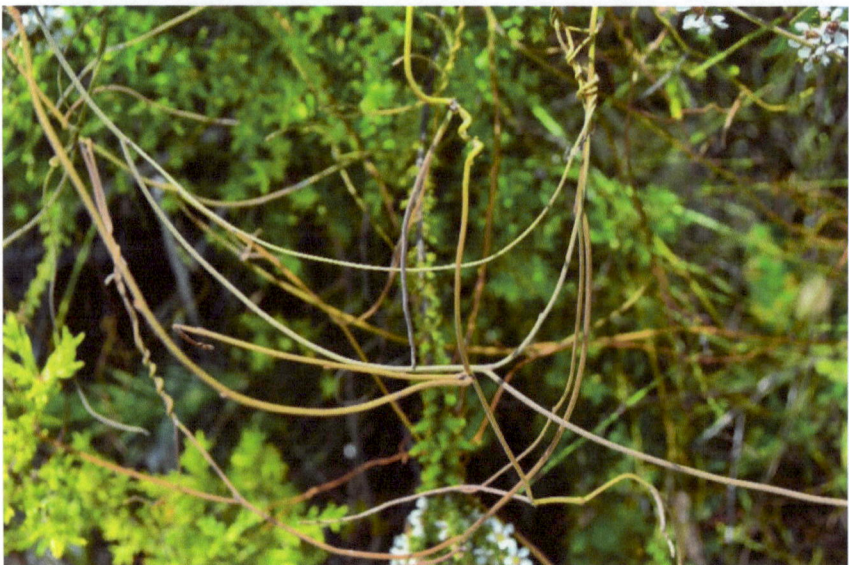

Dwarf Yellow-Eye
(*Xyris juncea*)

Other name: Hatpin

Identifying features: The Dwarf Yellow-Eye is a **perennial** herb. The bright yellow 3-petaled flowers of this species appear throughout spring and summer, growing singularly on stalks which reach approximately 50 cm in height. The flowers burst from brown egg-shaped flower heads, with each petal measuring between 5 and 9 mm long.

The leaves which cluster at the base of the flower stalk are flat, measuring 2.5-3 cm long and 1 mm wide. The seeds of this species are oval – **elliptic** in shape and measure between 0.3-0.6 mm long.

General notes: The term '*Xyris*' means 'cutting knife, or shears', while '*juncea*' means 'rush-like', a reference to the leaves of this species.

Frogsmouth
(*Philydrum lanuginosum*)

Other name: Woolly Waterlilies

Identifying features: The Frogsmouth is an aquatic, herbaceous **perennial** species, which can reach up to 2 m in height.

The spongy **linear**-shaped leaves of this species are between 30-80 cm in length and up to 20 mm wide. Between 12-25, mostly hairy, leaves generally emerge from the base of the plant, giving it a tufted appearance.

The bright yellow flowers of the Frogsmouth successively appear in spring and summer along a hairy green spike, with each flower bud enclosed by a woolly modified leaf (bract). When the buds mature, the bract reflexes and 'holds' the flower open. Each flower consists of 2 large outer petals (8-10 mm long), which are hairy on the outside, and 2 smaller inner petals, which surround the reproductive organs.

The hairy fruit produced by this species is approximately 10 mm long and 4-5 mm wide. They contain multiple reddish-coloured seeds up to 0.9 mm long.

General notes: The common name 'Frogsmouth' comes from the yellow flowers produced by this species looking like the mouth of a frog when open.

The Frogsmouth has a fibrous root system, which anchors it to the bottom of its muddy wallum environment.

Heathy Parrot Pea
(*Dillwynia retorta*)

Other name: Small-Leaf Parrot Pea; Twisted Parrot Pea

Identifying features: The Heathy Parrot Pea is an erect **evergreen** shrub of straggly appearance. It produces wiry branches, with younger plants displaying hair along the stems. When mature, this species attains heights up to approximately 3 m.

The smooth needle-like leaves of the Heathy Parrot Pea are **alternate**, between 4 and 12 mm long and spirally twisted.

Masses of bright yellow flowers with a red centre appear in winter and spring.

The plump purple-black seed pods which follow are 4-7 mm long, 4 mm wide and covered in hairs. The seeds contained within are smooth and released immediately when they mature, or within 1-2 days.

General notes: The scientific name of '*Dillwynia*' is in honour of Lewis Weston Dillwyn, a British Botanist. The Latin '*retorta*' means 'turned or twisted', a reference to the leaves of this species.

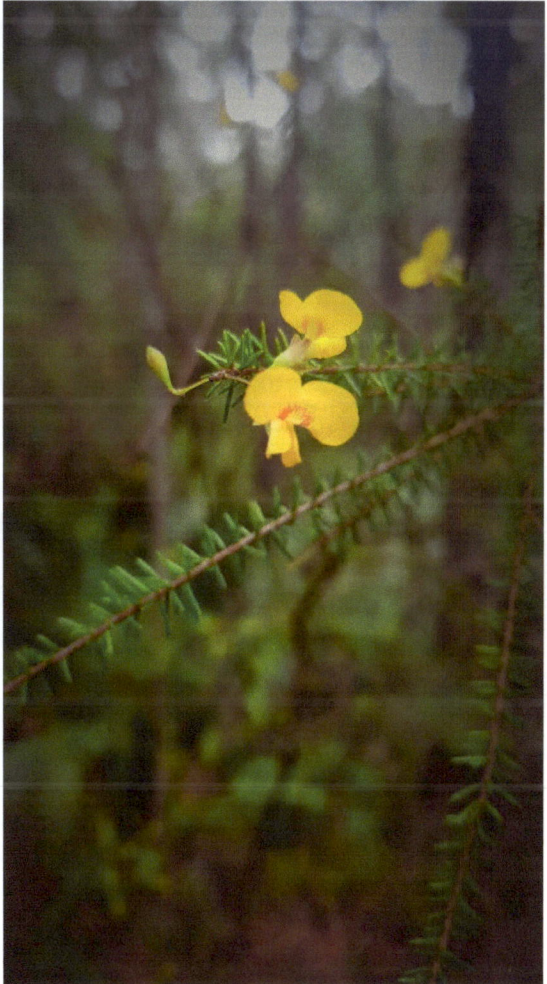

Leafless Milkwort
(*Comesperma defoliatum*)

Identifying features: The Leafless Milkwort is an erect, slender shrub which grows from a woody **rhizome** and reaches between 40-60 cm in height. The **elliptic**-narrow **elliptic**-shaped leaves of this species are 5-12 mm long and up to 1.5 mm wide. They are arranged alternately and produced on the lower part of the hairless stem.

Flowering of this species occurs from November to May, with the 3-5 mm long, 3-petaled blueish-purple flowers similar in appearance to that of a pea plant (see *Common aotus*).

The seed capsules of the Leafless Milkwort are oval in shape and 7-11 mm long. The seeds contained within are plump and egg-shaped, 1.5 -2.5 mm in length and covered in fine hair.

General notes: The name '*Comesperma*' is derived from the Greek words 'come' (meaning 'hair') and 'sperma' (meaning 'seed') and relates to the covering of hair found on the seeds of this species.

Lemon-Scented Tea Tree
(*Leptospermum liversidgei*)

Other name: Swamp May; Olive Tea Tree; Lemon Tea Tree

Identifying features: The Lemon-Scented Tea Tree is an **evergreen**, erect shrub growing between 2 and 4 m in height, with a spread of up to 1 m. The narrow, bright green leaves of this species are 5-7 mm long and contain citronella oil, giving them a strong and distinct lemon scent when crushed.

Flowering occurs in spring and summer when 5-petaled white (or rarely, pink) flowers appear. Flowers are oval-shaped and up to 8 mm in diameter. Flowering is followed by the appearance of woody capsules containing numerous seeds.

General notes: The scientific name of this species stems from the Greek words 'leptos' (meaning 'thin') and 'sperma' (meaning 'seed'). The term 'liversidgei' honours Professor A. Liversidge, an English-born Chemist who co-founded the Australasian Association for the Advancement of Science.

Pouched Coral Fern
(*Gleichenia dicarpa*)

Other name: Wiry Coral Fern

Identifying features: The numerous fronds of the Pouched Coral Fern grow from a multi-branched **rhizome**. Each frond reaches up to 2 m in length and contains multiple bright green leaf-like growths called 'pinnae'.

The pinnae measure up to 4 cm in length and consist of small individual pouch-shaped growths called 'pinnules' (1-1.5 mm long). The pouches on the lower surface of the pinnules contain 2 small sporangia (see **sporangium**) from which the reproductive spores are released.

Spores are yellowish in colour, however will darken and become black when mature.

General notes: The common name of the Pouched Coral Fern refers to the pouch-like pinnules which contain reproductive spores.

The scientific name of this species honours German Botanist W.F. von Gleichen.

Additionally, the Greek term 'dicarpa' ('two fruit') refers to the 2 sporangia located in each pouch of the pinnae.

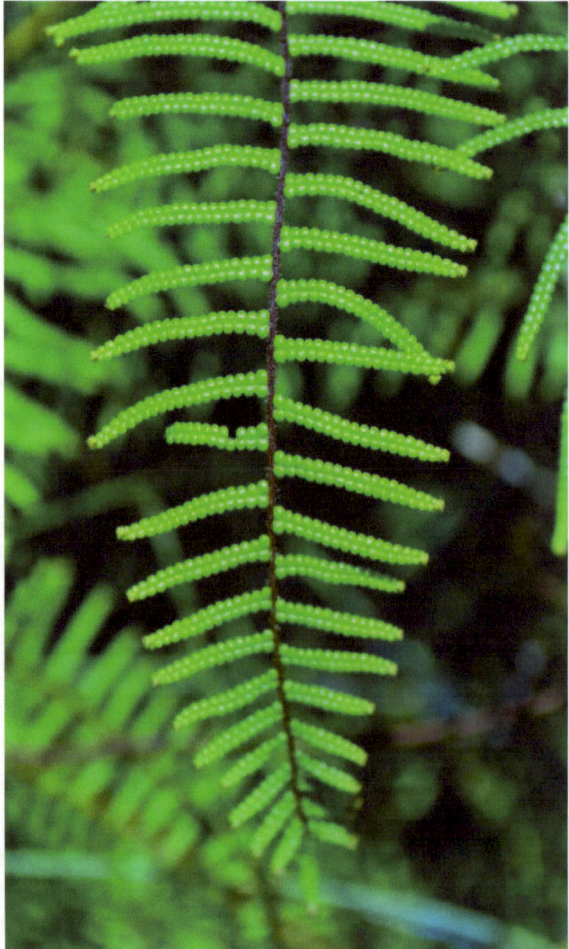

Saw-Toothed Banksia
(*Banksia serrata*)

Other name: Saw Banksia; Old Man Banksia

Identifying features: The Saw-Toothed Banksia is a small to medium-sized tree, often growing up to 16 m tall. The single, stout trunk of this species is habitually gnarled and covered in thick, grey, warty bark.

Leaves are **oblong** to **obovate**-shaped, between 7 and 20 cm in length and 2 to 4 cm wide, with serrated edges. The upper surface is dark green and glossy, while the under surface is light green.

The flower spikes are cylindrical-shaped, between 7 and 15 cm in height, up to 10 cm wide and produce hundreds of individual flowers grouped together. Colouration of the flower head is usually cream-grey, with flowering occurring during autumn and winter.

The seeds encased in the capsules of this species are approximately 3 cm long, brownish-black in colour and winged. The heat generated from fires opens the pods, whilst the resullting smoke encourages the seeds to germinate.

General notes: Banksias are able to re-grow after exposure to fire due to **epicormic buds** located underneath the bark.

Old flowers will remain on the plant for up to 7 years.

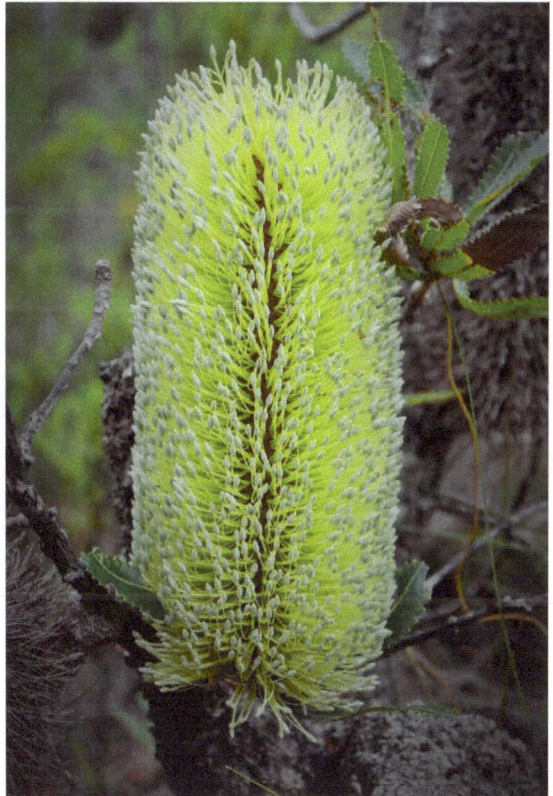

Showy Tea Tree
(*Leptospermum speciosum*)

Identifying features: The Showy Tea Tree is a dense shrub growing between 1-3 m in height, with a spread of up to 3 m. Bark colouration is red-brown and is often flaky in appearance. Younger stems have a soft covering of hair.

The leaves of this species are **alternate**, broad **lanceolate** to **elliptic** in shape and measure between 2-3 cm long and 5-10 mm wide. Young leaves have a fine covering of soft hairs.

The white 5-petalled flowers produced by the Showy Tea Tree appear in clusters from late winter to spring and are between 8-10 mm in diameter. The stamens measure approximately 1.5 mm in length. Following flowering tightly clustered 3-valved seed capsules which measure up to 5 mm in diameter appear.

General notes: The Showy Tea Tree is an important food source for various species of birds and insects (specifically, bees).

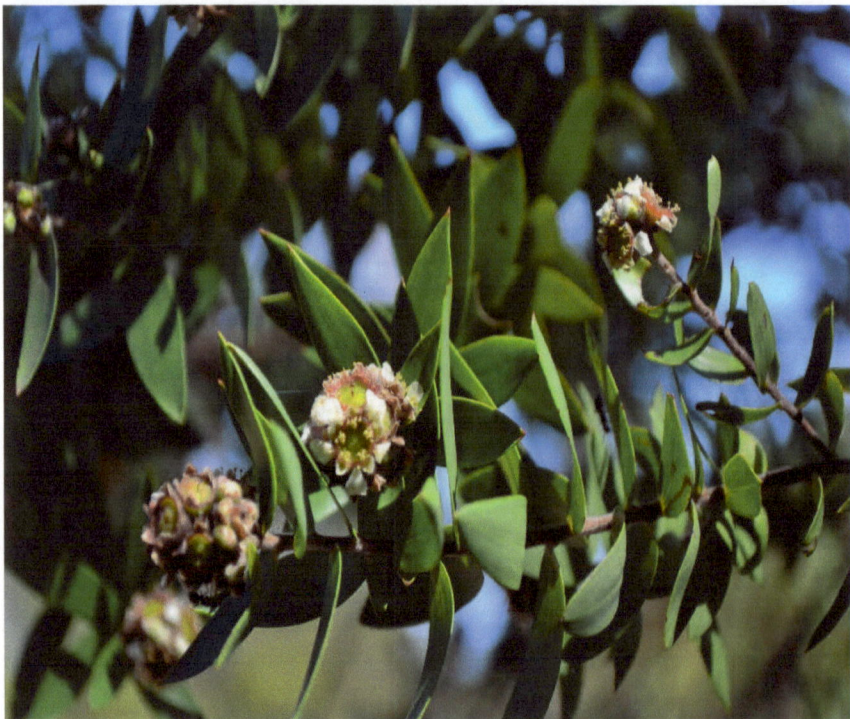

Small-Leaved Geebung
(*Persoonia virgata*)

Identifying features: The Small-Leaved Geebung is a medium sized shrub growing between 3 and 6 m in height.

It produces bright yellow, tubular-shaped flowers, whose petals curl backwards when mature. Flowering occurs in summer.

The leaves are **linear** in shape, up to 5 cm in length and 1-2 mm wide. They are bright green in colour and have a smooth texture. Young leaves often have a sparse covering of fine hair.

General notes: Small-Leaved Geebungs produce pale green fruit, between 7-20 mm in length, which contains a large seed. The fruits are edible and will fall from the tree when ripe. The taste of the fruit has been compared to that of a watermelon.

The fruit of this species was a popular food source for Fraser Island (K'Gari)'s Butchulla people.

Spoon-Leaf Sundew
(*Drosera spatulata*)

Other name: Common Sundew

Identifying features: The Spoon-Leaf Sundew is a small, carnivorous **perennial** plant which grows up to approximately 4 cm in diameter.

The spoon-shaped leaves of this species are attached to a central rosette by a broad flat stalk. Each leaf (including the stalk) measures up to 13 mm in length, 4 mm wide and produces multiple sticky tentacles which the plant uses to catch its insect prey.

White or pink flowers appear on erect, slender stems (which reach 8-24 cm high) from December to March. Between 3 and 15 individual 5-petaled flowers (up to 6 mm in diameter) occur along one side of the stem.

General notes: The scientific name of this species stems from the Greek word 'droseros' (which means 'dewy'). This refers to the sticky dewdrop-like fluid the leaf tentacles produce.

The Latin 'spatulata' refers to the spatula-shaped leaves.

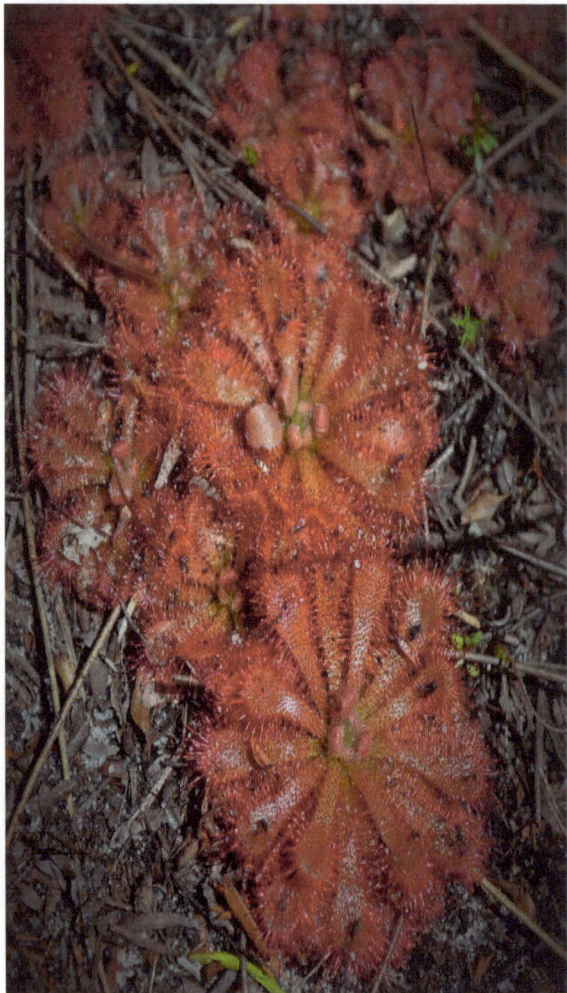

Swamp Banksia
(Banksia robur)

Other name: Broad-Leaved Banksia

Identifying features: The Swamp Banksia is a small to medium, straggly, **evergreen** shrub. This species grows between 2 and 3 m in height, with a spread of up to 2 m.

Leaves are large, (40 cm long, 12 cm wide), oval-shaped, tough and leathery with finely serrated edges. Colouration is dark green and glossy on the upper surface. The lower surface white and covered in fine hair. A yellow **midrib** runs the length of the leaves and is more prominent on the upper surface. New growth is covered in fine, brown hairs.

The flower spikes (10-17 cm high, 5-6 cm wide) appear in late spring and are initially blue-green in colour. When the flowers open, however, they turn yellow-green.

General notes: The first part of the scientific name of this species 'Banksia' is in honour of Sir Joseph Banks (see Coastal Banksia). The Latin 'robur' ('hard') refers to the hardness of its leaves.

Banksias can live for up to 100 years.

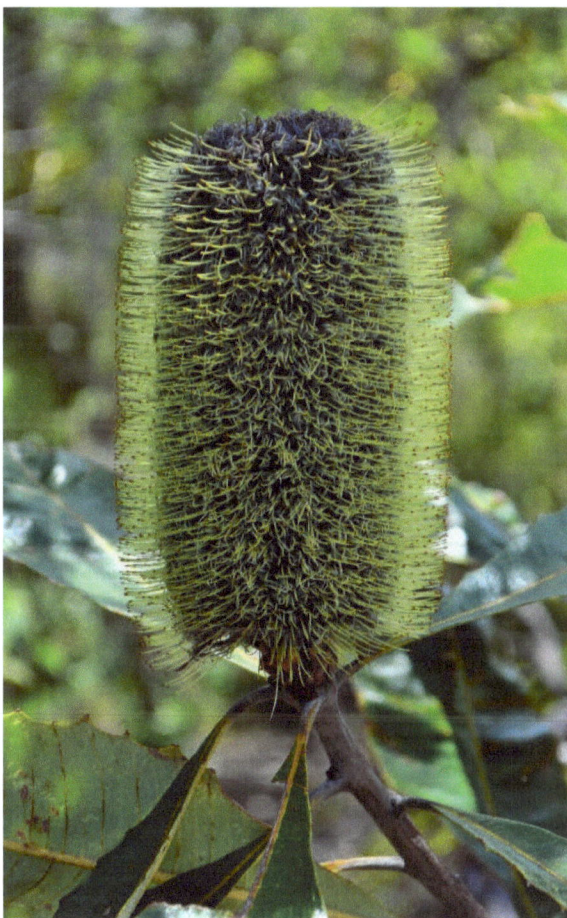

Swamp Grasstree
(*Xanthorrhoea fulva*)

Identifying features: The Swamp Grasstree is an herbaceous **perennial** shrub. This species lacks a distinct trunk, instead producing an underground branching stem. Leaves are long and grass-like, often blue-green in colour and up to 3.5 mm wide.

Flowering occurs between August and October (often stimulated by fire), with cream-coloured flower spikes (60 cm in height, 1-3 cm diameter) appearing atop woody stems between 0.2 and 1.6 m tall and 5-20 mm in diameter. Dull black **ovate**-shaped seeds are encased in multiple capsules produced along the flower spike, which split open to release the seeds when mature.

General notes: There are 28 species of Xanthorrhoea, all of which are endemic to Australia, with 3 species occurring on Fraser Island (K'Gari). They are *X fulva*, *X johnsonii* and *X macronema*.

Grasstrees provided many uses for the Butchulla people, including the nectar as a sweet treat, woody stems for spears and sap for resin.

Grasstrees can, reportedly, live for between 450-600 years.

Swamp Iris
(*Patersonia fragilis*)

Other name: Short Purple-Flag

Identifying features: The Swamp Iris is an erect **perennial** herb growing to a height of up to 80 cm. The twisted grey-green leaves grow from a short **rhizome**, which gives the plant a tufted formation. Leaves measure 15-80 cm in length and appear narrow (1-5 mm) and pointed.

Tubular (25-35 mm long) blue-purple flowers appear on stalks measuring up to 25 cm high from August to December. Each flower has 6 petals, consisting of 3 large outer lobes and 3 small lobes which are inner and erect. The outer petals measure 12-23 mm long, with the inner petals up to 2 mm in length.

The fruit produced by this species is a triangular-shaped 3-celled capsule (25-30 mm long) containing multiple oval-shaped seeds which change from cream to red-brown when mature.

General notes: More than 1 flower of an individual plant will rarely open at the same time.

Swamp Orchid
(*Phaius australis*)

Other name: Southern Swamp Orchid; Lesser Swamp Orchid

Identifying features: The Swamp Orchid is a large **evergreen** herb endemic to eastern Australia. It grows from a fleshy bulb-like structure and produces up to 8 large dark green leaves (50-125 cm in length; 80-100 cm wide), which narrow at the ends and form a tussock-like arrangement.

Thick stems up to 2 m in height bear between 4 and 16 large flowers (60-100 mm long; 65-110 mm wide) between August and December. The large sepals and petals of the flower are white on the outside and brown, with white veins, on the inside. The 3-lobed central tongue of the flower (the labellum) varies in colour from pink-purple and yellow. The flowers are long-lasting and open progressively from the lowest on the stem to the highest.

General notes: The Swamp Orchid is identified as 'Endangered' under both Queensland's Nature Conservation Act (1992) and the Australian Environmental Protection and Biodiversity Conservation Act (1999).

Sword Grass
(*Gahnia sieberiana*)

Other name: Red-Fruit Saw-Edge

Identifying features: Sword Grass is a tussock-forming **perennial** grass **endemic** to Australia. Large clumps measuring between 1-2 m in diameter and up to 2 m in height are common. The 1-2 m long leaves of this species are flat and rough with tiny, sharp serrations along the edges.

Clusters of black flowers appear along 3 m tall stems in spring and summer and are followed by small, shiny, orange-red seeds (2.5-4 mm long).

General notes: The scientific name of Sword Grass honours Botanists Henricus Gahn and Franz Sieber.

The seeds of this species appear to germinate after exposure to fire.

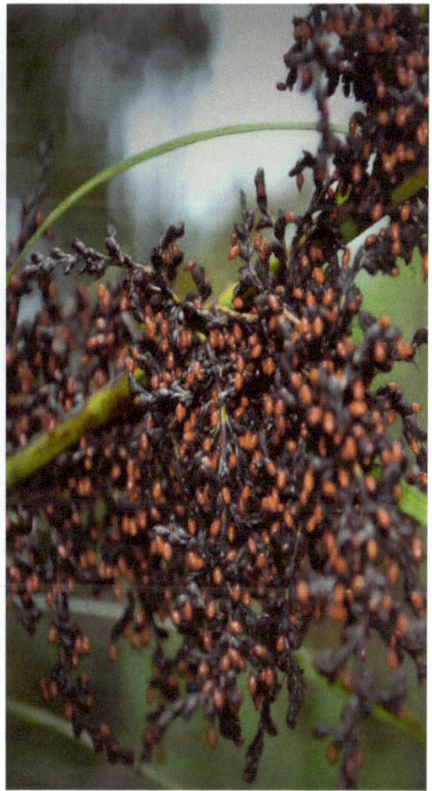

Wallum Banksia
(*Banksia aemula*)

Identifying features: The Wallum Banksia is a small to large **evergreen** shrub which grows between 3-8 m in height. The glossy green leaves are **obovate** to **oblong** in shape, serrated along the edges and measure between 3-22 cm in length and 1-2 cm wide. The bark of this species is orange-brown in color and warty and wrinkled in appearance.

Flowering occurs in autumn and early winter, with the green-yellow-coloured spikes (4-20 cm high, 8-9 cm wide) appearing from March to June. Over a 2 week period the multiple flowers open sequentially, from the bottom to the top of the spike.

General notes: Wallum Banksias are very similar in appearance to that of the Saw-Toothed Banksia. The Latin 'aemulus' means 'like' and refers to the similarities it shares with *Banksia serrata*.

The primary difference between the 2 species, however, is the shape of the **pollen presenter**. *Banksia serrata* produces a presenter which is long and narrow, whilst those of *Banksia aemula* are shorter and dome-shaped.

Six species of Banksia occur on Fraser Island, with Wallum Banksia the most common.

Wallum Heath
(*Epacris pulchella*)

Identifying features: The Wallum Heath is an erect shrub of slender appearance which grows to a height of between 75-150 cm. The small, stalkless leaves of this species measure up to 6 mm long and 1-4 mm wide. Their shape is **ovate**, tapering to a narrow and sharp point. Scarring occurs along the stems where leaves are removed from the plant.

Masses of 5-petaled white or pink tubular flowers appear throughout most of the year, however peak flowering occurs from January to May. The flowers measure between 5 and 8 mm in diameter. The fruit capsules which follow are small (2 mm in diameter) and contain multiple seeds. Colouration of the capsules is cream with rust-coloured tips.

General notes: The name of this species, *Epacris pulchella,* comes from the Greek words 'epi' (meaning 'upon') and 'acris' ('summit'). This refers to the habitat this species was originally thought to only occur in.

The Latin 'pulchellis' ('beautiful') refers to the attractive appearance of this species.

The flowers of the Wallum Heath produces abundant amounts of nectar, making it attractive to honey-eating bird species.

Water Snowflake
(*Nymphoides indica*)

Identifying features: The Water Snowflake is an **evergreen** aquatic **perennial** herb which grows in still or slow-flowing freshwater up to approximately 2 m deep. The majority of the plant is seen on the surface of the water, with the roots attached to the substrate below.

The flat, bright green leaves of this species are heart-shaped, 2-27 cm long, 2-25 cm wide and are produced on the ends of stems up to 2 m in length.

Multiple white flowers with yellow centres and delicate fringing on their petals appear on erect stems between 1-8 cm long between spring and autumn. The globular-shaped fruits of this species contain up to 50 round straw-coloured seeds measuring 1-2 mm in length.

General notes: The flowers produced by the Water Snowflake commonly have 5 petals, however they are known to have (rarely) had up to 7.

The fringing on the petals of the flowers increases surface tension and assists in preventing the flower from becoming submerged.

Wedding Bush
(*Ricinocarpos pinifolius*)

Identifying features: The Wedding Bush is a small to medium-sized shrub growing between 1-3 m in height. The leaves of this species are dark green, narrow and linear, 1-4 cm long and 1-3 mm wide.

Flowering occurs in winter and spring when masses of (usually) white star-shaped flowers appear. Both male and female flowers occur on the same plant, with 1 female flower often surrounded by 3-6 male flowers. The bright yellow stamens of male flowers differentiate them from females, which display a pale green ovary. Female flowers appear first.

The fruits of the Wedding Bush are a globular-shaped, spiny capsule up to 12 mm in diameter. When mature, the capsule splits open to release the multiple seeds inside.

General notes: The scientific name of the Wedding Bush comes from the Latin '*Ricinus*' (genus of the castor-oil plant) and 'carpos' (meaning 'fruit'), a reference to the fruit of this species being similar to that of the Castor-Oil plant. The Latin '*pinifolius*' refers to the pine-like leaves.

Weeping Coast Myrtle
(*Baeckea frutescens*)

Other name: Weeping Baeckea

Identifying features: The Weeping Coast Myrtle is a small to medium-sized shrub reaching 1-3 m high. The bark of this species is grey and often flaky. Branchlets hang in a downwards direction, giving the plant a 'weeping' appearance.

The small (4-10 mm long, 0.5 mm wide) needle-like leaves appear in clusters. They are linear in shape and green to greyish in colour when mature. Small white flowers appear from October to February. The petals of the flowers are rounded and measure up to 1.5 mm in length.

The non-woody fruits which follow are up to 2 mm in diameter, with each capsule releasing multiple small, flat, brown seeds when mature.

General notes: The scientific name of this species honours Dr Abraham Baeck, a Swedish Naturalist and best friend of Carl Linnaeus (the "father of modern taxonomy"). The Latin-derived *'frutescens'* refers to the shrubby appearance of this species.

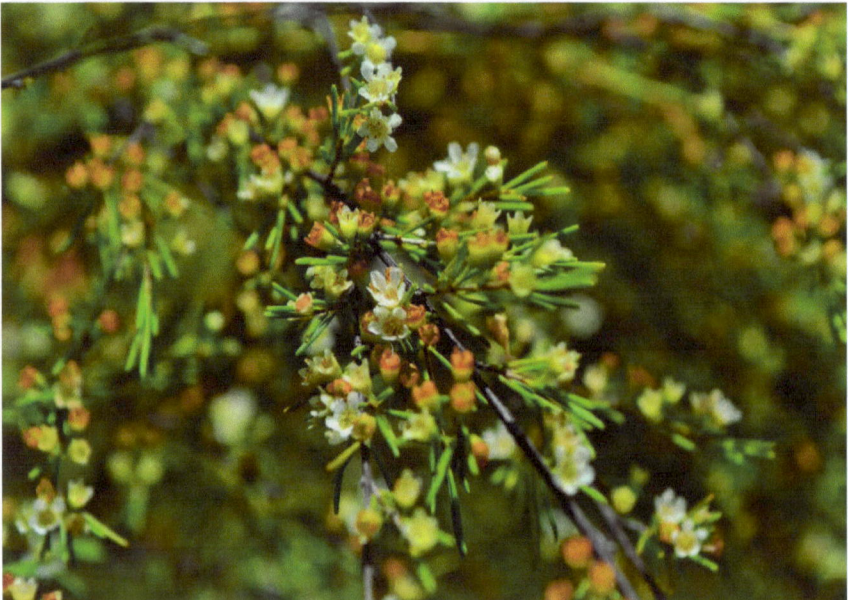

White Swamp Heath
(*Sprengelia sprengelioides*)

Identifying features: The White Swamp Heath is an erect shrub which grows up to approximately 1 m in height. The hairless stems of this species are wiry and smooth.

The glossy, bright green leaves are **ovate** in shape, up to 1.2 cm long, 3.2 mm wide and taper to a short, sharp point. They lack a distinct stalk, instead overlapping each other along the stem and are finely toothed on the margins.

Single white, tubular-shaped flowers 2-3 mm long, appear on the ends of branchlets during winter and spring. Each flower produces 5 erect or spreading petals, measuring up to 6 mm in length. The fruit which follows is up to 2.5 mm in diameter.

General Notes: The fruit of this species is an important food source for the ground parrot (*Pezoporus wallicus*).

There are 4 species of *Sprengelia*, with all of them being **endemic** to Australia. The White Swamp Heath however, is the only species found on Fraser Island (K'Gari).

Wide Bay Boronia
(*Boronia rivularis*)

Identifying features: The Wide Bay Boronia is a woody shrub which grows in an erect arrangement to a height of approximately 2 m. Its **compound** leaves measure between 1.7-6.8 cm in length and comprise 3-12 small **elliptic**-shaped leaflets (4-32 mm long, 1-5 mm wide). When crushed, the leaves emit a strong aniseed scent.

Flowering occurs in spring and summer when clusters of between 3 and 9 brightly-coloured pink flowers appear. Each of the 4 petals are up to 8 mm in length. Following flowering, flattened capsules 3-4 mm in length and up to 2.5 mm wide appear. When mature, the capsules release multiple small black seeds.

General notes: The scientific name of this species honours Francesco Borone, assistant to English Botanist John Sibthorp. The Latin '*rivularis*' means 'of a brook' and refers to the discovery of the first Wide Bay Boronia in a damp gully.

The Wide Bay Boronia is identified as 'Near Threatened' under Queensland's *Nature Conservation Act (1992)*.

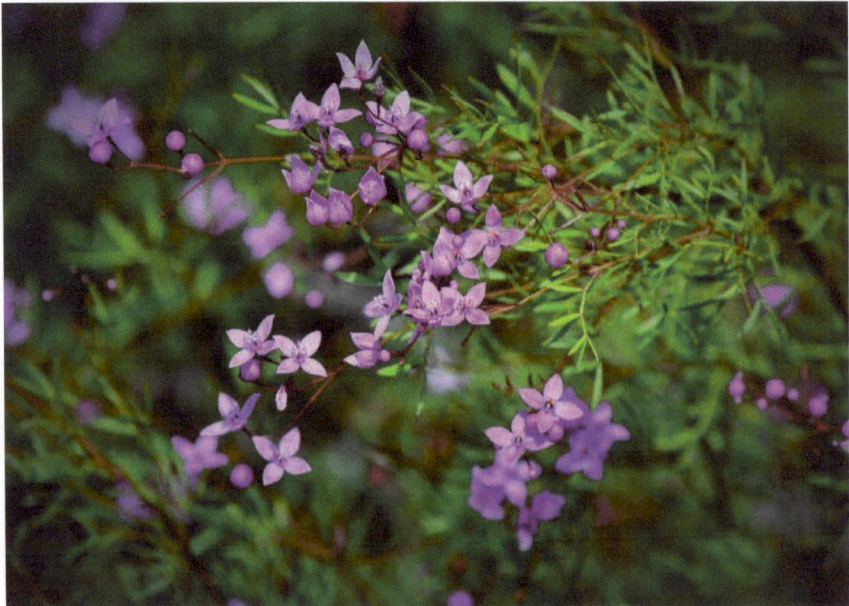

Willow Primrose
(*Ludwigia octovalvis*)

Other name: Shrubby Water Primrose; Raven Primrose Willow

Identifying features: The Willow Primrose is a **perennial** shrub, often with a woody base, which can reach a height of between 0.4-2 m. The leaves of this species are **lanceolate** in shape, between 1-15 cm long and 2-4 mm wide. Fine, pale hair is present on both the upper and lowers surfaces.

Flowering occurs throughout summer to winter, when solitary yellow flowers appear. Each flower has 4 spatula-shaped petals 1-2 cm long, underlain by 4 large green sepals (see **calyx**).

The Willow Primrose produces brown fruit 2-4.5 cm in length and 3-6 mm wide. When mature, the fruit splits open to release multiple small globular-shaped seeds.

General notes: The Willow Primrose appears to prefer moist areas such as freshwater wetlands or swamps, including billabongs and lakes.

Woolly Aotus
(*Aotus lanigera*)

Other name: Colden Candlesticks; Pointed Aotus

Identifying features: The Woolly Aotus is a densely branched, long-stemmed shrub, with stems densely covered in long, soft hairs. It can reach heights of up to 2 m and has a spread of approximately 1 m.

The small leaves of this species are bright green, 1-2.5 cm long, 2-4 mm wide, with slightly curved margins and grow in an upright position parallel with the stem. The upper surface is generally smooth, however the lower surface often has fine soft hair.

Masses of stunning golden flowers appear throughout late autumn to spring. Red markings similar to other pea plant species are possible, but rare. The flowers produced are typically pea-shaped (see *Common Aotus)* and between 8-15 mm in length. The fruit pods of this species are **obovate** in shape, measure up to 1 cm in length and are covered in masses of fine hair.

General notes: The Woolly Aotus, as per other pea plants, is a 'nitrogen fixer' (see *Black Casuarina*).

Yellow Pea Bush
(*Phylotta phylicoides*)

Other name: False Parrot Pea; Heath Phylotta

Identifying features: The Yellow Pea Bush is an erect shrub reaching up to 1 m in height. It's reddish-coloured stems, particularly in the upper parts of the plant, are covered in fine, soft hairs.

The bright green leaves of this species are narrow-**linear** in shape, between 6-15 mm long and 1-2 mm wide. The margins of the leaves curl underneath and there is often a small hook on the tip.

Clusters of bright yellow pea-shaped flowers (see *Common Aotus*) with red markings appear towards the ends of crowded leafy branchlets from August to October.

Leaf-like structures called bracteoles grow between the 5-12 mm long flowers, which curve at the tip. The fruit pods produced by this species measure 5 mm long and are covered in fine hair.

General notes: The Yellow Pea Bush was first described in 1837 by English Botanist George Bentham, often described as "the Premier systematic botanist of the 19th Century".

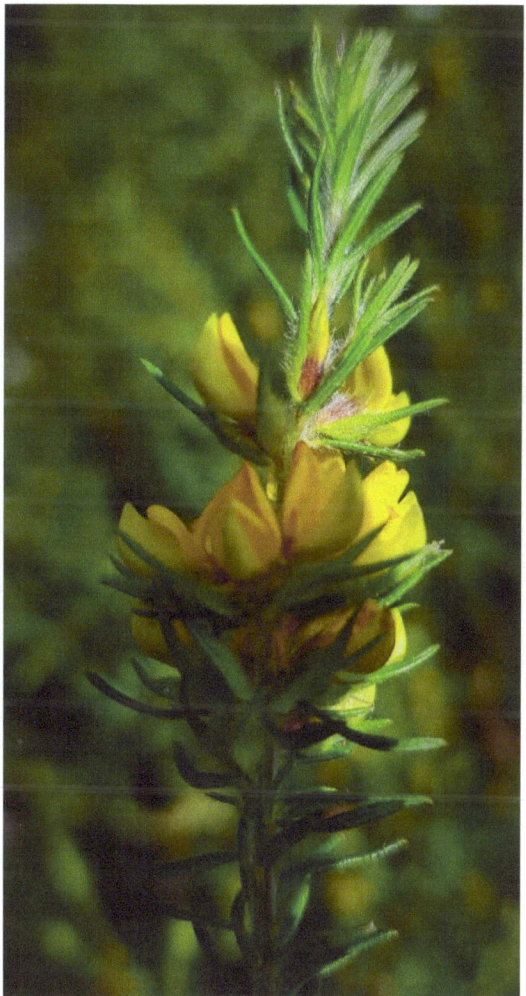

Yellow Tea Tree
(*Leptospermum polygalifolium*)

Other name: Tantoon

Identifying features: The Yellow Tea Tree is a shrub between 3-4 m in height with a spread of up to 3 m. The bark of this species is rough, with younger stems often covered in short, soft hairs.

The bright green leaves are **oblong**-shaped, between 5 and 20 mm long and 1-5 mm in width. The margins can be either flat or slightly curved, with a narrowing of the leaf at the tip. When crushed, they release a slight citrus scent.

Throughout August to January this species produces spectacular displays of white, 5-petaled flowers between 1-1.5 cm in diameter. Each petal is rounded in appearance and measures 4-6 mm long. The multiple **stamen** rise above the petals, with a simple style (see **carpel**) emerging from the centre of the ovary. The fruit which follows flowering is a woody, multi-valved capsule 5-10 mm in diameter.

General notes: The Yellow Tea Tree was first described in 1797 by British Botanist, Richard Salisbury, from a Port Jackson specimen.

GLOSSARY OF TERMS

Accretion	Growth through the external addition of new matter.
Adventitious roots	Roots growing from an area of the plant other than the root zone (eg. the stem).
Alluvial	Soils composed of sediment transported and deposited by a flowing stream or river.
Alternate leaves	A single leaf attached at a node.
Anaerobic	A situation / environment in which oxygen is not present.
Astringent	Bitter or slightly acidic in taste or smell.
Calyx	The individual outer protective leaves of a flower bud, called 'sepals', are collectively termed the 'calyx'.
Carpel	Female reproductive organ of flowering plants. Consists of an ovary, style and a stigma (the receptive surface for pollen grains).
Catkin	A downward hanging flower spike.
Compound leaves	A leaf consisting of several distinct parts (ie. leaflets) joined to a single stem.
Deciduous	The annual shedding of leaves undertaken by some plant species.
Dioecious	Unisexual – male and female reproductive organs on different individuals (separate male and female plants).
Ecology	The study of the relationships between an organism and its surrounding environment.
Ecosystem services	The benefits people obtain from ecosystems.
Ecotone	An area of transition between 2 plant communities.

Elliptic	The broadest part of an elliptic leaf is the middle, with the ends of the leaf narrowing equally. The total length of the leaf is approximately twice as long as it is wide.
Endemic	Restricted to a certain area / region due to factors such as isolation or climate.
Epicormic bud	A bud beneath the bark of a plant from which new growth will emerge. Epicormic buds remain dormant until they are activated by certain conditions (eg. fire).
Epiphyte	A plant that uses another plant for physical support, without deriving water or nourishment from it.
Erosion	The transportation of particles (soil or rock) due to weathering from water, wind and moving ice.
Evergreen	Plants which retain their green leaves all year.
Flanging	Swelling which occurs at the site where a branch attaches to the trunk of a tree. Provides mechanical support to the branch. Visible in woody plants.
Haustoria	A modified stem or root of a parasitic plant which penetrates the tissues of its host to access nutrients and water.
Hemiepiphtye	A plant that spends part of its life cycle as an epiphyte.
Hemiparasite	A plant that derives its nutritional requirements from another living plant.
Hypersaline	An aquatic environment that is saltier than typical seawater.
Lanceolate	Leaves which are significantly longer than they are wide, with the widest part of the leaf occurring below the middle. The end of the leaf tapers to a point.

Lignotuber	A swelling at the base of some plant species. Provides protection against destruction (fire) and stores food and buds from which new growth can sprout.
Linear	Leaves which have parallel margins and are more than 12 times longer than they are wide.
Midrib	The central (usually thick) structure running through the middle of a leaf from the base to the tip. Its function is to provide support for the leaf and to transport food and water into the leaf.
Monoecious	Both male and female reproductive organs in the same individual; hermaphrodite.
Morphology	The form and structure of an organism.
Natural selection	The process by which environmental factors (climate, disease, competition, food availability) determine the survival of individual members of a species. Often referred to as 'Survival of the Fittest'.
Needle-like	Leaves which resemble needles.
Node	The place on a plant stem to which leaves attach.
Oblong	Leaves resembling a rectangle in shape, except with rounded corners of the leaf. They are twice as long as they are wide.
Obovate	Leaves similar in shape to an egg. The broader end of the leaf is the one furthest from the stem.
Operculum	Lid or cover.
Opposite leaves	A pair of leaves attached at a node.
Ovate	Leaves similar in shape to an egg. The broader end of the leaf is the one nearest the stem.

Parasite	An organism that lives in, or on, an organism of another species and obtains benefits such as nutrients and water at the expense of its host.
Perennial	Plants that live for more than two years.
Photosynthesis	The process by which green plants use light energy, carbon dioxide and water to create chemical energy (plant food).
Phyllodes	Modified leaf stems which look and function like leaves.
Pioneer species	A plant that appears early in vegetational succession. These plants possess characters such as rapid growth and many small, easily dispersed seeds, which enable them to establish on open sites.
Pneumatophore	A specialised aerial root used for gas exchange (oxygen, carbon dioxide).
Pollen presenter	The style and stigma of flowers in the plant family Proteaceae onto which pollen is attached and 'presented' to pollinators such as birds or insects.
Propagules	Structures which become detached from a plant, giving rise to a new plant (bud, spore).
Re-afforestation	The replanting of a forest species which have been depleted due to, for example, logging.
Rhizome	A horizontally creeping underground stem which bears roots and leaves.
Saprophyte	A plant, microorganism or fungus which survives on dead, or decaying, matter.
Symbiosis	The living together of two organisms of different species in permanent, or prolonged, close association with beneficial or negative consequences for at least one of the organisms.

Spatulate leaves	Leaves which are broadly round at the tip, gradually curving towards the base.
Sporangium	A structure in which the reproductive spores of species, such as ferns, are formed. Typically found on the underside of leaves. Plural: sporangia.
Stamen	Male reproductive organ of flowering plants. Consists of a stalk, or filament, bearing the anther where pollen is produced.
Storm surge	When sea level is temporarily raised above its normal height as a result of wind stress and reduced atmospheric pressure during storms.
Toothed leaves	The margin of the leaf is jagged.
Transpiration	The evaporation of water through the stomata of plant leaves and stems.
Whorled leaves	Three or more leaves attached at a node.

INDEX

Coastal

Beach Evening Primrose (*Oenothera drummondii*) 20.

Beach Spinifex (*Spinifex longifolius*) 21.

Coastal Banksia (*Banksia integrifolia*) 22.

Coastal Jack Bean (*Canavalia rosea*) 23.

Coastal She-Oak (*Casuarina equisetifolia*) 24.

Goats Foot Vine (*Ipomoeapes caprae*) 25.

Knobby Club-Rush (*Ficinia nodosa*) 26.

Native Pig Face (*Carpobrotus glaucesens*) 27.

Pandanus Screw Palm (*Pandanus tectorius*) 28.

Twining Guinea Flower (*Hibbertia scandens*) 29.

Mangroves

Grey Mangrove (*Avicennia marina*) 33.

Orange Mangrove (*Bruguiera gymnorhiza*) 34.

Red Mangrove (*Rhizophora stylosa*) 35.

Tall Eucalypt Forest

Blackbutt (*Eucalyptus pilularis*) 38.

Moreton Bay Ash (*Corymbia tessellaris*) 39.

Narrow-Leaved Scribbly Gum (*Eucalyptus racemosa*) 40.

Pink Bloodwood (*Corymbia intermedia*) 41.

Queensland Blue Gum (*Eucalyptus tereticornis*) 42.

Smooth-Barked Apple (*Angophora leiocarpa*) 43.

Swamp Mahogany (*Eucalyptus robusta*) 44.

Rainforest

Blue Tongue (*Melastoma affine*) 48.

Brush Box (*Lophostemon confertus*) 49.

Bush Cherry (*Syzigium australae*) 50.

Cinnamon Myrtle (*Backhousia myrtifolia*) 51.

Common Silkpod (*Parsonia straminea*) 52.

Hairy Psychotria (*Psychotria loniceroides*) 53.

Hoop Pine (*Araucaria cunninghamii*) 54.

Kauri Pine (*Agathis robusta*) 55.

King Fern (*Angiopteris evecta*) 56.

Lemon Myrtle (*Backhousia citriodora*) 57.

Native Gardenia (*Atractocarpus fitzalanii*) 58.

Native Violet (*Viola hederacea)* 59.

Picabeen Palm (*Archontophoenix cunninghamiana*) 60.

Red-Fruited Palm Lily (*Cordyline rubra*) 61.

Satinay (*Syncarpia hillii*) 62.

Staghorn Fern (*Platycerium superbum*) 63.

Strangler Fig (*Ficus watkinsiana*) 64.

Swamp Lily (*Crinum pedunculatum*) 65.

Tallow Wood (*Eucalyptus microcorys*) 66.

White Beech (*Gmelina leichhardtii*) 67.

Zamia Palm (*Macrozamia douglasii*) 68.

Mixed Forest

Black She-Oak (*Allocasuarina littoralis*) 71.

Blueberry Ash (*Elaeocarpus reticulatus*) 72.

Bracken Fern (*Pteridium esculentum*) 73.

Bungwall Fern (*Blechnum indicum*) 74.

Bushy White Beard (*Leucopogon margarodes*) 75.

Cypress Pine (*Callitris columellaris*) 76.

Flax Lily (*Dianella revoluta*) 77.

Forest Boronia (*Boronia rosmarinifolia*) 78.

Foxtail Sedge (*Caustis blakei*) 79.

Heath Platysace (*Platysace lanceolata*) 80.

Hop Bush (*Dodonaea triquetra*) 81.

Johnson's Grasstree (*Xanthorrhoea johnsonii*) 82.

Midyim Berry (*Austromyrtus dulcis*) 83.

Mistletoe (*Amyema sp.*) 84.

Narrow-Leaf Platysace (*Platysace linearifolia*) 85.

Prickly Broom Heath (*Monotoca scoparia*) 86.

Prickly Moses (*Acacia ulicifolia*) 87.

Primrose Ball Wattle (*Acacia flavescens*) 88.

Showy Guinea Flower (*Hibbertia linearis*) 89.

Sickle Wattle (*Acacia falcata*) 90.

Slender Rice Flower (*Pimelea linifolia*) 91.

Spotted Hyacinth Orchid (*Dipodium variegatum*) 92.

Woombye (*Phebalium woombye*) 93.

Wallum

Broad-Leafed Paperbark (*Melaleuca quinquenervia*) 97.

Cape Blue Water Lily (*Nymphaea caerulea*) 98.

Common Aotus (*Aotus ericoides*) 99.

Dodder Vine (*Cassytha filiformis*) 100.

Dwarf Yellow Eye (*Xyris juncea*) 101.

Frogsmouth (*Philydrum lanuginosum*) 102.

Heathy Parrot Pea (*Dillwynia retorta*) 103.

Leafless Milkwort (*Comesperma defoliatum*) 104.

Lemon-Scented Tea Tree (*Leptospermum liversidgei*) 105.

Pouched Coral Fern (*Gleichenia sp.*) 106.

Saw-Toothed Banksia (*Banksia serrata*) 107.

Showy Tea Tree (*Leptospermum speciosum*) 108.

Small-Leaved Geebung (*Persoonia virgata*) 109.

Spoon-Leaf Sundew (*Drosera spatulata*) 110.

Swamp Banksia (*Banksia robur*) 111.

Swamp Grasstree (*Xanthorrhoea fulva*) 112.

Swamp Iris (*Patersonia fragilis*) 113.

Swamp Orchid (*Phaius australis*) 114.

Sword Grass (*Gahnia sieberiana*) 115.

Wallum Banksia (*Banksia aemula*) 116.

Wallum Heath (*Epacris pulchella*) 117.

Water Snowflake (*Nymphoides indica*) 118.

Wedding Bush (*Ricinocarpos pinifolius*) 119.

Weeping Coast Myrtle (*Baeckea frutescens*) 120.

White Swamp Heath (*Sprengelia sprengelioides*) 121.

Wide Bay Boronia (*Boronia rivularis*) 122.

Willow Primrose (*Ludwigia octovalvis*) 123.

Woolly Aotus (*Aotus lanigera*) 124.

Yellow Pea Bush (*Phylotta phylicoides*) 125.

Yellow Tea Tree (*Leptospermum polygalifolium*) 126.

BIBLIOGRAPHY

Anderson, C 2004, *Fraser Explorer Tours Interpretive Manual*, Kingfisher Bay Resort & Village, Fraser Island.

Atlas of Living Australia 2019, https://www.ala.org.au/

Australian Institute of Marine Science 2018, *Mangroves – more than*, https://www.aims.gov.au/docs/projectnet/mangroves-more-than.html

Australian Museum 2019, *The Mesozoic Era*, https://australianmuseum.net.au/learn/dinosaurs/mesozoic-era/

Australian Native Plants Society 2019, *Wallum and coastal heathland study group*, http://www.anpsa.org.au

Beach Protection Authority of Queensland 1990, *Coastal sand dunes – their vegetation and management*, Brisbane, Queensland.

Calvert G & Liessmann L 2014, *Wetland Plants of the Townsville–Burdekin Flood Plain*, Lower Burdekin Landcare Association Inc., Ayr.

Coastal Gardens – a planting guide for the Fraser Coast region n.d., Fraser Coast Regional Council, Hervey Bay, Queensland.

Davie, P 1998, *Wild guide to Moreton Bay*, Queensland Museum, Brisbane.

Davies, C & Price, J n.d. , *Waterplant guide – A guide to help ranger groups with the 'waterplants' section of the I-Tracker Cape York Rapid Wetland Assessment*, https://www.nespnorthern.edu.au/wpcontent/uploads/2015/10/waterplant_guide_web.pdf

De Micco, V & Aronne, G 2012, 'Morpho-anatomical traits for plant adaptation to drought', in R. Aroca (ed.), *Plant responses to drought stress*, Springer-Verlag, Berlin.

Department of Agriculture & Water Resources 2016, *Australian forest profiles – Eucalypt*, Department of Agriculture & Water Resources, Canberra.

Department of the Environment, Water, Heritage and the Arts 2009, *Ecosystem Services: Key Concepts and Applications, Occasional Paper No 1*, Department of the Environment, Water, Heritage and the Arts, Canberra.

Environmental Protection Agency 2003, *Fraser Island world heritage area - review of outstanding universal value*, Brisbane, Queensland.

Environmental Protection Agency 2005, *Great Sandy Region Management Plan (1994 – 2010)*, Revised Version 2005, Brisbane, Queensland.

Evans, L (ed) 2014, *Wallum wildflower guide for the Bundaberg region.* Bundaberg Regional Council, Bundaberg, Queensland.

Fennessy, B 2005, *What's in a name?*
https://www.friendsanbg.org.au/sites/default/files/pdf/bernardpapers.pdf

Fraser Coast Regional Council n.d., *Weed control of Fraser Island – guidelines for settlements of Fraser Island*, Fraser Coast Regional Council, Hervey Bay, Queensland.

Fraser Island Defenders Organisation 2018, *A history of FIDO and its campaigns – past and present - the end of logging and the world heritage listing (backgrounder)*,
http://fido.org.au/moonbi/backgrounders/02%20History%20of%20FIDO.pdf

Fraser Island Defenders Organisation 2018, *Fraser Island's flora (backgrounder)*,
http://fido.org.au/moonbi/backgrounders/27%20FI%20Flora%20Backgrounder.pdf

Fraser Island Defenders Organisation 2018, *Geomorphology*,
http://fido.org.au/about-fraser-island/geomorphology/

Gill, MA 2005, *How fires affect biodiversity*, Centre for Plant Biodiversity Research, http://www.anbg.gov.au/fire_ecology/fire-and-biodiversity.html

Greig, D 1998, *A photographic guide to trees of Australia*, New Holland Publishers, Sydney, Australia.

Hope, C & Parish, P 2008, *A wild Australia guide to native plants*, Steve Parish Publishing, Brisbane, Queensland.

Horak, M, Day, MF, Barlow, C, Edwards, ED, Su, YN & Cameron, SC 2012, 'Systematics & biology of the iconic Australian scribbly gum moths *Ogmograptis* Meyrick (Lepidoptera: Bucculatricidae) and their unique insect-plant interaction', *Invertebrate Systematics*, vol 26, pp. 357-398.

Hornsby Shire Council n.d., *Allocasuarina littoralis – black oak [fact sheet]*, Hornsby Shire Council, NSW. https://www.hornsby.nsw.gov.au/_resources/documents/environment/idigenous-trees/Fact-sheet-Allocasuarina-littoralis-Black-Oak.pdf

Hornsby Shire Council n.d., *Eucalyptus racemosa - narrow-leaved scribbly gum [fact sheet]*, Hornsby Shire Council, NSW. http://www.hornsby.nsw.gov.au/media/documents/environment-and-waste/bushland-and-biodiversity/native-tree-database-fact-sheets/Fact-sheet-Eucalyptus-racemosa-Narrow-leaved-Scribbly-Gum.pdf

James, SA, Smith, WK & Vogelmann, TC 1999 'Ontogenetic differences in mesophyll structure and chlorophyll distribution in *Eucalyptus globulus* spp. *globulus* (Myrtaceae)', *American Journal of Botany*, vol. 82, no. 2, pp. 198-207.

Kingfisher Bay Resort & Village 2004, *Rangers Department Nature Notes*, Kingfisher Bay Resort & Village, Fraser Island.

Kingfisher Bay Resort & Village 2018, *Plants list at Kingfisher Bay Resort, Fraser Island.* https://www.kingfisherbay.com.au

Knox, B, Ladiges, P & Evans, B 1997, *Biology*, McGraw-Hill, Sydney, Australia.

Masood, M, Downing, A, Downing, K, & Atwell, B 2014 *Native ginger – Alpinia caerulea [fact sheet]*, Department of Biological Sciences, Macquarie University, Sydney, NSW file:///C:/Users/JACINTA/Downloads/Plant%20of%20the%20week%20-%20Alpinia%20caerulea%20-%20Native%20Ginger.pdf

Milne, L n.d., *Tour Plan – Bush tucker*, Kingfisher Bay Resort & Village, Fraser Island.

Milne, L n.d., *Tour Plan – Wallum*, Kingfisher Bay Resort & Village, Fraser Island.

Milne, L n.d., *Tour Plan – Wildflowers*, Kingfisher Bay Resort & Village, Fraser Island.

Noosa's Native Plants 2018, *Noosa's Native Plants*, Noosa, Queensland, www.noosasnativeplants.com.au

Padgett, J 2004, *Tour Plan – Beaches*, Kingfisher Bay Resort & Village, Fraser Island.

Padgett, J 2004, *Tour Plan – Mangroves*, Kingfisher Bay Resort & Village, Fraser Island.

Queensland Parks and Wildlife Service 2013, *Fire management – managing parks and forests [brochure]*, Department of National Parks, Recreation, Sport and Racing, Brisbane, Queensland.
Sheather, W, & Sheather, G 2017, *Dipodium punctatum, Hyacinth orchid*,

Australian Plants Society of New South Wales. https://austplants.com.au/Dipodium-punctatum-Hyacinth-Orchid

Walmsley, C 1995, *Bush tucker – a guide to Fraser Island's edible plants*, Kingfisher Bay Resort & Village, Fraser Island

ACKNOWLEDGEMENTS

I would like to gratefully acknowledge and thank the following people for the help and assistance they have provided me throughout the development of this book:

Liz Stephens, Melissa Haigh, Peter Meyer, Russell Keeton, Ruth Thomas, Shane Edmondstone, Sienna Keeton, Toni Jackson and the members of the Queensland Plant Identification Group.

"In the end we will conserve only what we love; we will love only what we understand; and we will understand only what we are taught"
Baba Dioum, 1968

ABOUT THE AUTHOR

Jacinta developed her love for Fraser Island (K'Gari) when she began working there in 2004 as an Interpretive Guide. Her interest further developed through her later work as a Conservation Officer with Queensland Parks and Wildlife Service.

Spending her days introducing visitors to the amazing flora and fauna of the island, as well as to the island itself, instilled a deep and ever-lasting passion for this remarkable natural wonder. She is an enthusiastic environmental educator and enjoys sharing her knowledge of ecosystems with others.

Jacinta strongly believes that engaging with the natural world is the key to conservation and sustainability. She hopes that other people experiencing the beauty and uniqueness of places such as Fraser Island (K'Gari) will be motivated to conserve and protect our declining natural areas.